The Internet and the Google Age: Prospects and Perils

Edited by Dr Jonathan D. James

Edith Cowan University, Australia

Research-publishing.net

Research-publishing.net

Published by Research-publishing.net, not-for-profit association
Dublin, Ireland; Voillans, France, info@research-publishing.net

The Internet and the Google Age: Prospects and Perils
Edited by Dr Jonathan D. James, Edith Cowan University, Australia

Typeset by Research-publishing.net
Cover illustration and design by Raphaël Savina
Icons cover: https://github.com/Templarian/MaterialDesign
License Icons - SIL Open Font License 1.1

ISBN13: 978-1-908416-16-2 (Paperback - Print on demand, black and white)
Print on demand technology is a high-quality, innovative and ecological printing method; with which the book is
never 'out of stock' or 'out of print'.

ISBN13: 978-1-908416-17-9 (Ebook, PDF, colour)
ISBN13: 978-1-908416-18-6 (Ebook, EPUB, colour)

Legal deposit, Ireland: The National Library of Ireland, The Library of Trinity College, The Library of the
University of Limerick, The Library of Dublin City University, The Library of NUI Cork, The Library of NUI
Maynooth, The Library of University College Dublin, The Library of NUI Galway.

Legal deposit, United Kingdom: The British Library.
British Library Cataloguing-in-Publication Data.
A cataloguing record for this book is available from the British Library.

Legal deposit, France: Bibliothèque Nationale de France - Dépôt légal: novembre 2014.

Notes on Contributors

The Editor

Jonathan D. James, Ph.D., is a researcher and writer on media, religion and culture. His research interests include: cultural globalization, the social effects of new media, new religious movements, indigenization, and diaspora Asians in the West. He is currently an adjunct lecturer at Edith Cowan University in Perth, Australia and oversees a church-based development and training organization in the Asia-Pacific region. He is the author of *McDonaldisation, Masala McGospel and Om Economics: Televangelism in Contemporary India* (Sage, 2010) and editor of *A Moving Faith: Mega Churches go South* (Sage, forthcoming, November, 2014).

The Reading Committee

Assoc. Prof. Panizza Allmark is the program director in Communications at the School of Communications and Arts, Edith Cowan University, Australia and general editor of *Continuum: Journal of Media & Cultural Studies*.

Prof. Michael J. Day is a professor of English at Northern Illinois University, USA and co-editor of the book *The Online Writing Classroom* (2000).

Dr Joyce E. James was formerly a visiting associate professor in Linguistics at the National Institute of Education in Nanyang Technological University, Singapore and editor of the *RELC Journal*. She is the author of *Grammar in the language Classroom* (SEAMEO, 2003).

Dr Beate Josephi is an adjunct lecturer in the School of Communications and Arts, Edith Cowan University, Australia and author of *Journalism Education in Countries with Limited Media Freedom* (2010).

Prof. Sudakar Reddy is professor and head of the Centre for Folk Culture Studies, University of Hyderabad, India. He is the editor of *FOSSILS* (Folklore Fellows of South Indian Languages) and serves on the editorial boards of *Folklore Journal of South Indian Folklorist* and *Indian Folklore Research Journal*.

The Authors

Michael Jaffarian, a researcher with World-Venture (formerly the Conservative Baptist Foreign Mission Society), is a senior research associate with Operation World. He served for six years as executive director of the Singapore Centre for Evangelism and Missions and for seven years as an editorial associate for the *World Christian Encyclopedia*, second edition (Oxford University Press, 2001).

Nicola F. Johnson, Ph.D., is a senior lecturer in the School of Education, Gippsland, Victoria, in the Faculty of Education and Arts of the newly established Federation University, Australia. Her research interests include Internet over-use, technological expertise and the use of digital technologies within formal and informal spaces of learning. She is the author of two books: *The Multiplicities of Internet Addiction: The Misrecognition of Leisure and Learning* (Ashgate, 2009), and *Publishing from your Ph.D.: Negotiating a Crowded Jungle* (Gower, 2011).

Iremae D. Labucay is a senior survey analyst at Social Weather Stations (SWS), a non-stock, non-profit, social research organization in the Philippines. She has presented papers at international conferences and symposiums including the World Association for Public Opinion Research (WAPOR) conference held in Amsterdam, the Netherlands.

Carmel O'Reilly has recently completed an online module in Technology Enhanced Learning Teaching and Assessment (TELTA) at level 9 as a component of the MA in Education with the Learning Teaching and Technology Centre at Dublin Institute of Technology (DIT). She has been researching Mind Mapping as an eLearning tool for the enhancement of learning. She is currently assistant lecturer with DIT specialising in French as a foreign language. Her research interests include Culinary French and French film and food. Her most recent publication, *À table: An exploration of the uses of food in Jean Renoir's La Grande Illusion, 1937*, appears in the journal of Food & History, Food & History, volume 11, issue 1.

Anne Rice, Ph.D., graduated with a BSc. in Sociology and MSc. in Communications in 1997. Since then, she has worked for several years in the community and voluntary sectors. She has extensive experience in managing a wide-range of research projects, such as, emigration research, art therapy research, community audits and feasibility studies. As an independent researcher, Anne is particularly interested in the role of new technologies such as social media in rural communities.

Paul Emerson Teusner, Ph.D., completed his graduate studies at the School of Media and Communication at RMIT University in Melbourne. His research explored how people used blogging to negotiate relationships within local communities and online networks in their construction of religious identities. Paul currently manages youth services in a not-for-profit organization in Melbourne. His research interests include how Cyborg Theory may inform us on how young people use mobile devices in their presentations of gender, family and tribe.

Etáin Watson is a lecturer in Italian in the School of Languages, Law and Society at Dublin Institute of Technology, Dublin, Ireland. She is a graduate of the University of Dublin, Trinity College, the University of Sussex and University College Dublin. Her research interests are in the use of technology and media in foreign language teaching, Italian film studies and Irish and Sardinian folklore. She has presented papers at conferences in Italy, Spain, Ireland and Albania and has published peer reviewed papers and book chapters in Ireland, the U.S., Italy, Spain and Iran.

Acknowledgements

This book would not have been possible without the assistance and encouragement of several institutions and people.

I thank the wonderful contributors for their concise and thought-provoking studies. It's been a real pleasure to collaborate with each one of you.

I'm grateful to Edith Cowan University and Dr John Hall for providing valuable editorial support.

The preparation of the manuscript for typesetting was in the capable hands of Avrille Wasserman; and I appreciate her labor of love.

I'm deeply indebted to the editorial committee for reading the chapters and offering helpful suggestions along the way.

To Sylvie Thouësny and the team at Research-publishing.net, I offer sincere appreciation for all your hard work in coordinating this project.

Finally and most importantly, I thank my wife Elizabeth and children Ben and Mel for their support, assistance and prayers in enabling me to complete this task.

While every effort has been made to give the proper attribution to all the sources mentioned in the book, if we have inadvertently omitted anyone, we would love to have the opportunity to make the necessary amendments.

Dr Jonathan D. James

Table of Contents

Table of Contents

The Internet and the Google age: Introduction[1][2]

Jonathan D. James[3]

Imagine a world in which every single person on the planet is given free access to the sum of all human knowledge (Jimmy Wales, founder of Wikipedia).

---

1.   Introduction

The World Wide Web celebrated its 25th anniversary on the 12th of March 2014, having radically transformed the way we socialize, work, shop and engage in politics. Central to the critical role played by the Internet is its access to information resources. Never in the history of mankind has there been such an opportunity to access virtual libraries on a plethora of subjects in real time. And search engines like Google offer an ever-increasing array of information. This, along with the constant improvements in technology, ensures that information sources and social networking opportunities via the Internet are "exponentially increasing" (Edwards & Bruce, 2002, p. 180).

Research by the Mccrindle Group reveals some startling statistics about 'generation z', those born between 1995 and 2009, and 'generation alpha', those born after 2010 (Mccrindle website, 2014). Worldwide, there are more than 5 billion Google searches per day (hence we are living in the Google Age)

---

1. I use the word Internet (upper case), to refer to "the world-wide network of computer networks [...] that operate using a standardized set of communications protocols called TCP/IP (transmission control protocol/Internet protocol). An internet (lower case) is a network of smaller computer networks" (The Linux Information Project website, n.d.).

2. Our focus in entitling the book The Google Age is to show the ubiquity of Google, the Internet's largest search engine and not necessarily to focus on Vaidhyanathan's (2011) thesis in his book: The Googlization of Everything, a reference to Google's "techno-fundamentalism" ideology (p. 3).

3. E-mail address: aefi@iinet.net.au

How to cite this chapter: James, J. D. (2014). The Internet and the Google Age: Introduction. In J. D. James (Ed.), *The Internet and the Google age: Prospects and perils* (pp. 1-25). Dublin: Research-publishing.net. doi: 10.14705/rpnet.2014.000175

---

and more than 500 million tweets[1] per day, mostly from but not restricted to generation z (Mccrindle website, 2014). However, the downside to this activity is the need for 'googlers' and 'tweeters' to sort treasure from trash (Tillman, 2003).

In this introductory chapter, I begin by looking at the Internet from an historical and communication perspective in an effort to understand its significance in the contemporary world. I then give an overview of the most searched topics on the Internet and identify prospects that have opened up and perils that lurk in the information highways of our Internet age. I conclude with a brief overview of the chapters in this volume of studies.

2. Historical overview and significance

It is important to view the Internet age historically, because every major technological revolution in the past has impacted communication. Communication scholar Innis predicted in 1949 that "it is difficult to overestimate the significance of technological change in communication or the position of monopolies built up by those who systematically take advantage of it" (Innis, 1949, p. 47).

The pre-modern world was characterized by face-to-face communication, thus most people were confined to family and village circles, and human interaction was the only means of communication. The invention of the printing press in the 15th Century, which later led to newspapers, brought a major change with 'line by line', propositional communication, written in words. The invention of the telephone, and then the radio, added new dimensions as communication was aurally relayed through sound waves. The invention of film and television

---

1. The word 'tweets' comes from the sounds made by birds. However, with the launch of Twitter, an online micro-blogging site, 'tweet' means an online post written by a Twitter user with 140 characters or less. The post usually gives a running commentary of what the person has been doing, their future plans, and other personal information either serious or trivial in nature.

married the senses of sight and sound and brought about another phase in the communication revolution[1].

Today, we have the Internet –probably the most exciting phase of communication, which is based on digital technology. In digital technology, data is expressed as a series of digits starting from the number '0' onwards, whereby "text, graphics, audio and video can be easily transmitted over the Internet or computer networks" (BusinessDictionary.com website, n.d.).

What makes this contemporary Internet age different from the communication of previous ages? I have identified six characteristics.

2.1.   Immediacy

Mehrabian (1967, 1971), while illustrating interpersonal communication, described immediacy in terms of how certain aspects of communication behaviour, especially non verbal aspects, can enhance physical and psychological closeness:

> "People are drawn toward persons and things they like, evaluate highly, and prefer; and they avoid or move away from things they dislike, evaluate negatively, or do not prefer" (Mehrabian, 1971, p. 1).

Immediacy is expressed in terms of speed and psychological factors, allowing the meaningful exchange of information through email, Facebook, Twitter, Instagram, blogging and a host of technological platforms. Furthermore, virtual communities are being formed through common interests and desires. For example, social media sites allow people to join networks with relative ease and swiftness, a reality that was unimaginable in previous generations.

Adam Kramer, a social scientist and one of the many Facebook researchers working with Facebook said that in the past "he would have had to get papers

---

1. For a thought-provoking analysis of how communication technology shapes and is shaped by social processes, read Flichy (1995).

published and then hope that someone noticed. At Facebook, 'I just message someone on the right team and my research has an impact within weeks, if not days'" (cited in Albergotti, 2014, p. 25).

Just like academic research, news on the Internet is made available almost instantaneously (MDIA1001 website, n.d.). Today's technology, located at our fingertips allows for breaking news and events to be posted online, seconds after they occur. According to De Wolk, "News is like bread – it is best served fresh and quickly goes stale" (cited in MDIA1001 website, n.d.). In keeping with this adage, more and more people are accessing news online because they want it fresh and fast. According to a UK-based study, Communications Market Report, "over 48 percent of 24-34 year olds use the Internet to keep up with news, and one in five trust that websites contain accurate and unbiased content" (Ofcom website, 2010).

This response is typical of how today's generation get their news:

> "On the day that King of Pop Michael Jackson died just over a year ago, I didn't find out from reading the newspaper, nor did I find out from any online news website. I found out through the many status updates on Facebook and Twitter. I read more about it through links to blogs and websites that were holding their own cyberspace memorial service. I didn't once question the authenticity of this shocking update; I somehow figured that if everyone was talking about it, it should be true" (MDIA1001 website, n.d.).

Contemporary journalism is built on the premise that news should be disseminated to the public as soon as possible and the Internet helps fulfill this as an immediate platform. However, does immediacy in regard to news and journalism come at the expense of accuracy? What is the priority among today's generation z?

Another matter of concern is that the sense of immediacy that pervades the Internet age gives us little room to reflect and weigh up the pros and cons in any given situation because emails, Facebook invitations and the like come with the expectation of instant responses. These, no doubt, are areas for contemporary researchers to grapple with.

2.2. Interactivity and participation

The Internet is by definition an interactive medium between networks of computer users (Rust & Varki, 1996), and the primary means for interactivity is the availability of user–generated content (UGC), which is described as:

> "any form of content such as video, blogs, discussion [...] posts, digital images, audio files, and other forms of media [...] created by consumers or end-users of an online system or service and is publically [sic] available to other consumers and end-users" (Webopedia website, n.d.).

Jenkins (2009) asserts that the Internet makes it increasingly easier for ordinary citizens to publish and distribute information to multiple audiences. He uses a word coined by Toffler (1980), 'prosumers', to refer to contemporary individuals who have blurred the traditional lines between producers and consumers of content (Jenkins, 2006, p. 38). Hence Internet users are no longer just passive consumers because they can just as easily participate by being producers – YouTube being an excellent example of this.

And part of this shift in news journalism is the emergence of 'citizen journalists' –ordinary people who contribute to news making. Citizen journalism is a reference to the

> "countervailing ethos of the ordinary person's capacity to bear witness, thereby providing commentators with a useful label to characterize an ostensibly new genre of reporting" (Allan, 2009, p. 18).

Jenkins (2009) also introduces another term, 'participatory culture', to depict the way people create and share content that inspires the participants:

> "Participatory culture is emerging as the culture absorbs and responds to

the explosion of new media technologies that make it possible for average consumers to archive, annotate, appropriate, and recirculate media content in powerful new ways" (Jenkins, 2009, p. 8).

With this shift comes a new sense of power for the everyday citizen hitherto reserved for the 'gatekeepers': professional journalists and broadcasters.

The 2004 Tsunami disaster was a significant time frame in the popularity and acceptance of user-generated content (Allan, 2009). The new genre of citizen journalism or "crowdsourcing" (obtaining data and information from the public) challenged traditional journalism throughout the world because the stories and footage about the tsunami used by media outlets were produced by tourists and ordinary citizens on site (Akagi & Linning, 2013; PeaceWork website, 2006). Media outlets were therefore dependent on 'amateur' content for their media coverage of the unfolding drama. Media scholars recognize 2004 as a turning point: "Never before has there been a major international news story where television crews have been so emphatically trounced in their coverage by amateurs wielding their own cameras" (cited in Allan, 2009, p. 18).

Since the tsunami, a string of media events relied heavily on amateur content: the 2005 London bombings, Arab Spring (2010 onwards)[1], Occupy Wall Street (2011)[2], Kony 2012[3] and the Boston Marathon bombing (2013). Media analysts share these extraordinary statistics of the London bombings:

"On the day of the London bombings, the BBC received more than 1,000

1. A series of political uprisings that began in the Middle East starting with Tunisia and moving into Egypt, Syria, Libya and other nations.

2. Occupy Wall Street (OWS) is the name given to a protest movement that was launched in the financial district of New York City, USA in 2011. Organized by an anti-globalization and anti-consumerist group, the OWS slogan, "We are the 99%" refers to the unequal distribution of wealth in the USA compared to the 1% representing the rest of the world. The protests gained media attention both in the traditional media agencies and on the Internet and social networking sites. For a fuller treatment on this movement read, "Occupy Movement: Does the protest movement against inequality have staying power?" in CQ Researcher (2012). Retrieved from: http://www.sagepub.com/ritzerintro/study/materials/cqresearcher/77708_8.1cq.pdf

3. Kony 2012 is a half-hour documentary that exposes Joseph Kony –a warlord in Uganda allegedly "responsible for the enslavement of more than 30,000 children" (News.com website, 2012). The documentary was intentionally produced to get the attention of various Internet platforms such as YouTube in order to reach a global audience (News.com website, 2012).

photographs, 20 pieces of amateur video, 4,000 text messages, and 20,000 e-mails, all in the first six hours" (Anbarasan, 2007, p. 266).

The volume and presumed accuracy of information from the public has prompted the traditional media outlets like the BBC to change the rules of engagement and embrace community expression.

It is believed that during the Boston Marathon bombings, an iPhone photograph taken by a citizen journalist provided a clear image of one of the suspects which later led to the arrest of the perpetrator in question (Akagi & Linning, 2013).

The public participation phenomenon is both amazing and convincing, but there is a downside: self-mediation has entered the equation, and there is the possibility that truth may now be compromised.

In education, online learning, interactivity and participation are changing the structure of traditional education. There are several studies that show a nexus between a positive online environment and the overall learning experience (Rovai, 2002; Wegerif, 1998). Furthermore, collaboration with faculty and other students can be a strong impetus for learning (Johnson & Johnson, 1999). Online teachers are encouraged to provide a helpful online presence, together with useful content delivery (Palloff & Pratt, 1999). The relational dynamics in the online setting have indeed taken on a new direction with the launch of the *Open University* concept in various countries, which could lead to exponential growth in all aspects of education. The University of the future could be one without classrooms, walls and borders.

A study where students were assessed on the quality of articles they submitted online to Wikipedia for an Economics assignment revealed that the students' writing quality improved (Freire & Li, 2014). Furthermore, significant improvements occurred in the overall discipline of writing with the inclusion of strong, primary sources and an overall willingness to follow up on feedback from Wikipedia editors (Freire & Li, 2014).

Nicola Johnson describes in chapter 7 how the Internet, by virtue of its egalitarian nature, is changing the traditional structures of information and knowledge, privileging a new echelon of 'experts' and IT gurus.

The rapid increase of Internet users and consequently, increased interactivity, have resulted in the amazing growth of business 'start ups' such as eBay, Facebook, Google and Amazon. These businesses are built on the principle of interaction. Facebook combined with Twitter have already enjoyed the reputation of toppling government regimes, introducing brands, creating campaign awareness and raising money for charities.

2.3.   Visualization

Most web pages on the Internet use infographics, which is data presented in visual form. Ofcom in the UK report that the Google Image Search ("Google's sister search site") has become "a significant search engine in its own right" compared to Google's own main web search, and "other general search engines such as Bing, Yahoo and MSN portal" (Ofcom website, 2010). YouTube, a vast online video channel, although not listed in the Ofcom study, is a massive platform for visualization. According to the Mccrindle Group, there are 4 billion YouTube searches listed worldwide per day (Mccrindle website, 2014). From Youtube you can learn how to do bungee jumping, play the guitar, or wear a sari. So this is not the usual classroom 'sit and listen' approach. It could be argued that the majority of YouTube users are seeking entertainment rather than education; nevertheless we recognize new vistas opening up for visual learners. Visual learner Aimee Boucher, now a visual teacher, shares her methodology:

> "To help me support visual learners (and other learning styles), I use the strategy *teach around the wheel.* Teaching around the wheel refers to using multiple modalities throughout your lesson in an effort to present content using students' preferred modality. Students develop a deeper understanding of important concepts when information is present using a variety of modalities" (Boucher, 2011, para 3).

Boucher (2011) then goes on to list specific web 2.0 tools[1] besides YouTube, that support and challenge visual learners: Glogster, Google Earth, Spezify, GoAnimate, Bubble.us, Prezi, Microsoft Movie Maker and Photostory 3. Flickr, yet another visual tool, is an online photo management and sharing site where a logged-on user can view photographs taken by people all over the world and also create online albums to share with others.

A noteworthy aspect of searching the web is the principle of Search Engine Optimization (SEO). SEO is the process of optimizing the chances that a particular site or image will appear first in a list of searched-for topics. For example, a search for 'fishing' reveals images of all things related to fishing (still photographs, videos, animation etc.) as well as text-based fishing material. Naturally, people are more inclined to click on sites that display relevant images. News-based organizations such as CNN, BBC and Al-Jazeera are alert to this and have therefore created facilities to link up-to-date images in all their stories. By optimizing their ranking and because of the popularity of images over text, these organizations are reaping the benefits of attracting Internet traffic in the process.

Skype video conferencing is another popular platform, enabling people from any part of the globe to talk to each other in real time.

Google Earth, originally called EarthViewer 3D "is a virtual globe, map and geographical information program that was created by Keyhole, Inc, a Central Intelligence Agency funded company acquired by Google in 2004" (Wikipedia website, Google Earth, n.d.). Here are some specific features of this incredible online facility:

> "You can zoom and glide over stitched together satellite photos of the world. Use Google Earth to find driving directions, find nearby restaurants,

---

1. Web 2.0 is a reference to the upgraded technology of the Internet as opposed to Web 1.0 which is a "read only", static version of the Internet. Therefore Web 2.0 is described as a "read and write", interactive Internet. For more information see http://oreilly.com/web2/archive/what-is-web-20.html.

measure the distance between two locations, do serious research, or go on virtual vacations" (About.com Google website, n.d.).

Real time visualizations, like Google Earth, are powerful purveyors of reality and its technological wonders are yet to be fully realized. They surpass the quality of infographics and point to the Internet as the "living organism that it is" (Motherboard website, 2013).

2.4. Multiplicity of information sources

Whereas traditional textbooks remain a valuable source of information on any given subject, the Internet has multiple virtual 'textbooks' immediately on hand. And the information in these online texts goes far beyond textbook facts and figures to include the drama of real life experience, adventure and even experimentation. Online texts may not necessarily be written in a logical and sequential fashion following the traditional Euro-American models of epistemology. Stahl, Hynd, Britton, McNish, & Bosquet (1996) studied student learning experiences in the USA and found that using multiple-text sources are effective, but cautioned that users need to be taught the skills of using the vast array of materials effectively. Stahl et al. (1996) also revealed that users tend to choose short, well-constructed texts over lengthy documents.

Etáin Watson, in chapter 6 describes the effectiveness of Internet Search engines in advancing language acquisition and learning skills while Carmel O'Reilly illustrates in chapter 5 how Google searches are somewhat of a dilemma as there are both benefits as well as limitations, especially for students trying to sift through large amounts of information.

The most popular source of encyclopedic knowledge is Wikipedia, with its millions of articles that can be edited by any member of the public at any time. It is based on the concept that by using people's "brainpower and harnessing collective intelligence", the Internet can have a comprehensive encyclopedia that is constantly being updated (BBC website, n.d.).

Wikipedia platforms exist in the following languages: Spanish, Dutch, French, Polish, Chinese, English (nearly 4 million articles) Japanese, Italian and Portuguese (BBC website, n.d.). Wikipedia claims to have more than 80,000 contributors and has approximately 400 million visitors around the world each month (BBC website, n.d.).

Wikipedia and other websites use the tool of hyperlinks –a reference to the web commands in the various sites that allow you to jump to a related site. Every web page is filled with several hyperlinks, with each one sending you to a related website, picture or file:

> "Hyperlinking is the foundation of the web. As users add new content, and new sites, it is bound in to the structure of the web by other users discovering the content and linking to it. Much as synapses form in the brain, with associations becoming stronger through repetition or intensity, the web of connections grows organically as an output of the collective activity of all web users" (O'Reilly website, n.d.).

Whereas Wikipedia is a research encyclopedia for the common person, Google Scholar is a specialized search engine within Google Search to help scholars locate scholarly articles, theses, books, abstracts "from academic publishers, professional societies, online repositories, universities and other websites. Google Scholar helps you find relevant studies across the world of scholarly research" (Google Scholar website, n.d.).

Can every published work be conveniently catalogued in one website? This is the ambition of Google Books Library Project and Google World Catalog, a massive electronic catalog of the world's library:

> "We're working with several major libraries to include their collections in Google Books and, like a card catalog, show users information about the book, and in many cases, a few snippets – a few sentences to display the search term in context" (Google Books website, n.d.).

2.5.   Anonymity

Anonymity and pseudonymity are not exclusive characteristics of this digital age and, as can be seen in chapter 8, privacy is not guaranteed. An IP address[1] can be tracked, whereby the computer from which a certain post was made can be located, even though the actual user may not be that easily detected. However, by virtue of Internet technology it is easier for people to distribute anonymous and pseudonymous messages through email, chat rooms and blogging:

> "Sites such as Chatroulette and Omegle, which pair up random users for a conversation, capitalize on a fascination with anonymity. They are examples of anonymous chat or stranger chat. Other sites, however, including Facebook and Google+, require users to sign in with their legal names. In the case of Google+, this requirement has led to a controversy known as the nymwars" (Wikipedia, website, n.d.).

Palme and Berglund (2002) give an example of the above phenomenon by using a simple case involving emails:

> "[A] person sends an e-mail or writes a Usenet news article using a falsified name. Most mail and news software allows the users to specify whichever name they prefer, and makes no check of the correct identity. Using web-based mail systems like Hotmail, it is even possible to receive replies and conduct discussions using a pseudonym" (Palme & Berglund, 2002, section 5, para 2).

The online encyclopedia, Wikipedia, is a collaborative effort of many individuals who can remain anonymous, although all articles require unidentifiable pseudonyms or IP addresses.

A European Union Internet report (1999) shows that EU officials are aware of the issues surrounding anonymity, that is, the need for anonymity (especially in

---

1. IP refers to Internet Protocol. To connect with the Internet, a unique series of numbers is provided to each computer.

several repressive nations) and its inherent dangers; this is a reference to people who use the Internet for illegal activities (cited in Palme & Berglund, 2002).

What is perhaps more important in the discussion on anonymity is the online experience of users: users are known to experience a sense of pleasure and euphoria that they are entering a new realm anonymously and are involved in activities such as chatting, searching, gaming or researching. Psychological research by Suler (2004) reveals that people say and do things in cyberspace that they would not do in face-to-face communication. Just as some people socialize with an 'alcohol fix', when others enter cyberspace they "loosen up, feel more uninhibited, and express themselves more openly" (Suler, 2004, p. 323). This is called the 'disinhibition effect':

> "It's a double-edged sword. Sometimes people share very personal things about themselves. They reveal secret emotions, fears, wishes. Or they show unusual acts of kindness and generosity. We may call this *benign disinhibition.*

> On the other hand, the disinhibition effect may not be so benign. Out spills rude language and harsh criticisms, anger, hatred, even threats. Or people explore the dark underworld of the internet, places of pornography and violence, places they would never visit in the real world. We might call this *toxic disinhibition*" (Suler, 2004, p. 324).

2.6. Convergence[1]

A mobile or cellphone today is more than a simple device for making phone calls from one person to another. It is also a camera and an audio-visual recorder that can transmit images, text and sound to any number of people who are on the net. In short, convergence has taken place, which is explained in the following way:

---

1. Harry Jenkins (2008) sees convergence as a cultural rather than a technological process. The prospect of every "story, image, sound, idea and relationship being retold across different media channels tells us something about what we value today in our culture" (section 1, para 1).

"Media convergence is the merging [...] of previously distinct media to create entirely new forms of communication expression. Convergence is at the heart of today's digital media revolution and includes such technologies and software applications as the Internet and electronic commerce, smartphone technology, digital-film animation, DVD (digital video disc) music and high-definition television (HDTV), and video game systems to name only a few" (Gershon, n.d., para 1).

Digital technology is all about how data is transferred, be it text, images, sound and all the possible permutations. Instagram, an amazing new feature on Smartphones, is described as

"an online photo-sharing, video-sharing and social networking service that enables its users to take pictures and videos, apply digital filters to them, and share them on a variety of social networking services, such as Facebook, Twitter, Tumblr and Flickr" (Wikipedia website, Instagram, n.d.).

A prime example of convergence is Internet protocol television, IPTV, that is, the practice of watching TV on the Internet, a growing phenomenon with various brands in the market like Apple TV, FetchTV, Foxtel and GoogleTV offering this service (Brook, 2012). Research indicates that 30 percent of Australian residents in Sydney and Melbourne, aged between 25 to 54 years watch TV through the Internet (Brook, 2012).

If pre-modern culture was a 'hearing' culture and the modern world was a 'reading' and then a 'seeing' culture, the postmodern, Internet age, can be described as a 'multi-sensate' culture, where almost all the senses are called upon to engage in the activity of everyday living.

A recent report about the future of the Internet by the UK's national innovation agency; Technology Strategy Board predicts the future Internet as

"an evolving convergent Internet of things and services that is available anywhere, anytime as part of an all-pervasive omnipresent socio-economic fabric, made up of converged services, shared data and an advanced wireless and fixed infrastructure linking people and machines to provide advanced services to business and citizens" (MacManus, 2011, para 2).

Therefore, there is the likelihood that the Internet as we know it today will become more convergent, incorporating more diverse media and consequently increasing the richness of its characteristics. This will continue to challenge the traditional boundaries between private and public space, between home and work, and even between humans and non humans (robots).

3.   Internet use
and what people are searching

In all the morass of information, it may be helpful to pause and ask: what are people using the Internet for? Recent studies on what people want from the Internet show that users are "goal-oriented": they are not aimless 'surfers' but rather they wish to accomplish something specific online, such as information or association with other individuals or groups (Carton, 2000).

The Pew Research Center study in 2000 (as part of its Pew Internet and American Life Project) disclosed that people who use the net regularly are more in touch with their circle of friends and family than those who are not regular Internet users (Carton, 2000). This finding is 'fleshed out' in chapter 2, where Facebook is described as a tool to connect friends and families in transnational locations. Some other significant findings about Internet users in the Pew Study are[1]

- nearly 75 percent of users went online to search for information about their hobbies, or about purchases;

---

1. There is overlap in the usage, so the figures do not total up to 100 percent.

- 64 percent of respondents visited travel sites;

- 62 percent visited weather-related sites;

- over 50 percent did educational research;

- 54 percent were hunting for information about health and medicine;

- 47 percent regularly visited government websites;

- 38 percent researched job opportunities (Carton, 2000).

Pornography and religion seem to be two highly searched topics on the Internet. Whereas definitive studies in these two topics are not easily available, a few studies suggest that pornography is growing. As noted on Webroot website (2014),

- 25 percent of all search engine queries are related to pornography, or about 68 million search queries a day;

- 40 million American people regularly visit porn sites;

- 35 percent of all internet downloads are related to pornography.

The technology of convergence has made pornography more accessible: "data from the video porn website Pornhub –which had nearly 15 billion views in 2013– suggest that the adult entertainment sector is a leader in the shift to the mobile phone as well", that is, people are accessing pornography on their mobile phones (Online Services News website, 2013).

Also noteworthy is that in 2013, the USA "earned the distinction of being the first country tracked by Pornhub to watch the majority of its online 'porn' on mobile phones because about 52 % of 'porn' consumption was on mobile phones in 2013, compared to 46 % in 2012, making this significantly higher than anywhere else" (Online Services News website, 2013).

Users of the Internet may not be aware of the place religion occupies on the Internet. The Pew, Internet & American Life Survey's Cyberfaith reported responses of 1309 church-based congregations across the United States:

"Nearly two-thirds of online Americans use the Internet for faith-related reasons. The 64% of Internet users who perform spiritual and religious activities online represent nearly 82 million Americans. Among the most popular and important spiritually-related online activities measured in a new national survey: 38% of the nation's 128 million Internet users have sent and received email with spiritual content; 35% have sent or received online greeting cards related to religious holidays; 32% have gone online to read news accounts of religious events and affairs; 21% have sought information about how to celebrate religious holidays; 17% have looked for information about where they could attend religious services; 7% have made or responded to online prayer requests; and 7% have made donations to religious organizations or charities" (Hoover, Clark, & Rainie, 2004, pp. i-ii).

Paul Emerson Teusner reveals in chapter 3 how religion is establishing a presence on the Internet as faith is mediated for a largely post-modern audience. In line with this, Michael Jaffarian, in chapter 4, takes an extraordinary snapshot revealing how computer technology has advanced the mission of the Church.

4.   Perils

Studies by Buzzell (2005a) suggest that in comparison with other media such as theater, VCR and websites, Internet technology has made a difference in the access of pornography and accounts for its consequent higher use over recent years. Further studies by Buzzell (2005b) reveal the emergence of what he terms 'hyperpornography', a reference to how technology has "changed the variety, sophistication and means of the distribution of pornography to a wider market" (p. 112).

'Sexting', the practice of sending sexually explicit messages or images via cellphone or instant messenger has increased, not just among teens but also with adults (Hinduja & Patchin, 2010). The study shows that "the images are often initially sent to romantic partners or interests but can find their way into the hands of others, which ultimately is what creates the problems" (Hinduja & Patchin, 2010, para. 2).

Cyberbullying refers to individuals using 'stand over' tactics to disempower other people through the use of "digital technologies such as mobile phone text messages, emails, phone calls, internet chat rooms, instant messaging and social networking websites such as Facebook" (Ybarra & Mitchell, 2004, p. 325).

Cyberbullying is a fast growing trend and some experts "believe [it] is more harmful than typical schoolyard bullying" (Webster, n.d., para 1). Adolescent girls are named as the ones more at risk because they "are significantly more likely to have experienced cyberbullying in their lifetimes" (Hinduja & Patchin, 2013, p. 715).

Cyberbullying and sexting are not new social occurrences, but have gained attention due to the fact that in some cases these phenomena have led to suicides and the unceremonious fall from grace of some celebrities.

The Australian Institute of Criminology (2013) reveals that there is a marked increase in cybercrime over the last decade: "cybercrimes range from fraud, hacking, money laundering and theft, through to cyberstalking, cyberbullying, identity theft, child sexual exploitation and child grooming" (para 2).

The Infosec Institute, in their study of Cybercrime, reveals that close to 80 percent of cybercrime acts are based on organized activity (Infosec Institute Website, 2013). The study predicts, however, that with increased Internet penetration and skill development in users, new players not linked with organized crime could be attracted into Cybercrime as a business (Infosec Institute website, 2013).

According to Freedberg (2013), electronic warfare is the next phase of military research and development:

> "With their eyes on future adversaries more technologically sophisticated than the Taliban, commanders want new capabilities to shut down enemy electronic networks and protect their own. It's a challenge intimately interwoven with but distinct from the higher-profile field of cyber warfare...The [US] Army's Training and Doctrine Command (TRADOC) is drafting a new field manual for 'Cyber-Electromagnetic Activity'" (Freedberg, 2013, para 1-2).

The Internet is not without its dangers. However, on balance, it must be pointed out that ethical issues have always been around with or without technology so it is not technology *per se* that should be blamed for ethical problems. Today's technology has the potential to magnify moral and ethical issues.

5. Chapter summaries

This book seeks to explain the new digital world, 'warts and all'. It marvels at the benefits and notes the obstacles and threats involved in contemporary Internet usage.

Asia is poised to take the lead in the Internet revolution and so in chapter 1, Iremae Labucay zooms in on the Philippines (a nation whose citizens spend the highest share of time on Social Networking sites across world markets)[1] to seek an understanding of the particular patterns and habits of Internet users in this nation. The digital divide in the Philippines, as outlined in the chapter, is perhaps a reality in many developing nations around the world.

Social media and Facebook, one of the most successful business ventures of the Internet, is examined in chapter 2 as Anne Rice describes how it plays a role in

---

1. See http://www.comscoredatamine.com/tag/philippines/

maintaining family ties among the Irish *diaspora*. Interestingly, it also highlights the fact that in rural communities, by and large, the older males are unconnected to the Internet.

Chapters 3 and 4 pick up the point that was broached earlier, that religion is one of the most highly searched topics. Paul Emerson Teusner, in chapter 3, researches online religious advertising and how religious groups are repackaging the faith in ways that will attract members of generation z. Michael Jaffarian, in chapter 4, outlines in a narrative style, some astounding research breakthroughs that the Church has achieved in its efforts to reach the world through Internet technology.

The educational implications of the Internet are revealed in chapters 5 and 6 featuring French civilization (by Carmel O'Reilly) and Italian Studies (by Etáin Watson).

This is followed in chapter 7 with Nicola Johnson's use of the theoretical perspectives of French sociologist Pierre Bourdieu to explore how the Internet operates as a field, with several sub fields mediating knowledge and expertise and giving birth to a new set of non-hierarchical experts.

The book closes with chapter 8 which contains a summary of some of the ambiguities and pitfalls of the Internet age, such as how our privacy and confidentiality is impacted, and also how the Internet is looked upon with suspicion by certain nations with authoritarian ideologies. The chapter concludes with a quick snapshot of the Internet of the future.

6. Conclusion

We have progressed from several phases in the history of communication and technology –from an agrarian society to a manufacturing society and now, to a knowledge society where information has become the new currency of our time (James, 1992). Is it any wonder then that global agencies such as the World Bank allude to the fact that information literacy is the new key to unlock empowerment and learning in the knowledge society: "Knowledge accumulation and application have become major factors in economic development and are increasingly at the core of a country's competitive advantage in the global economy" (World Bank, 2002, p. xvii).

In essence, whether we like it or not, the Internet is here to stay –we are in the Google age. Furthermore, it seems likely that the future of our world depends on the Internet and all its offerings.

References

Akagi, K., & Linning, S. (2013, April 29). Crowdsourcing done right. *Columbia Journalism Review*. Retrieved from http://www.cjr.org/data_points/crowdsourcing_done_right.php

Albergotti, R. (2014, July 4). Facebook study poor: Sandberg. *The Australian*. Retrieved from http://www.theaustralian.com.au/business/wall-street-journal/facebook-study-poor-sandberg/story-fnay3ubk-1226976954342

Allan, S. (2009). Histories of citizen journalism. In A. Stuart Allan & E. Thorsen (Eds). *Citizen journalism: Global perspectives*. New York: Peter Lang.

Anbarasan, E. (2007). Citizen journalism and the new media. In N. Rajan (Ed). *21st century journalism in India* (pp. 265-274). New Delhi: Sage Publications.

Boucher, A. (2011, February 24). Technology and the visual learner. *Doing it Differently*. Retrieved from http://diwithtech.blogspot.com.au/2011/02/technology-and-visual-learner.html

Brook, S. (2012, May 5). The future is now for television viewing over the internet. *The Australian*. Retrieved from http://www.theaustralian.com.au/arts/review/the-future-is-now-for-television-viewing-over-the-internet/story-fn9n8gph-1226345020849?nk=b20c72206a34f9e336215cf055de153e

Buzzell, T. (2005a). Demographic characteristics of persons using pornography in three technological contexts. *Sexuality & Culture, 9*(1), 28-48. doi:10.1007/BF02908761

Buzzell, T. (2005b). The effects of sophistication, access, and monitoring on use of pornography in three technological contexts. *Deviant Behavior, 26*(2), 109-132. doi:10.1080/01639620590518988

Carton, S. (2000, May 24). What do people want online? *ClickZ*. Retrieved from http://www. clickz.com/clickz/column/1711156/what-do-people-want-online

Edwards, S. L., & Bruce, C. (2002). Reflective internet searching: An action research model. *The Learning Organisation, 9*(4), 180-188. doi:10.1108/09696470210428903

Flichy, P. (1995). *Dynamics of modern communication: The shaping and impact of new technologies*. London: Sage Publications.

Freedberg, S. J. (2013, November 25). Army electronic warfare goes on the offensive: New tech awaits approval. *Indian Strategic Studies*. Retrieved from http://strategicstudyindia. blogspot.com.au/2013/11/army-electronic-warfare-goes-on.html

Freire, T., & Li, J. (2014). Using Wikipedia to enhance student learning in economics. *Social Science Research Network*. Retrieved from http://ssrn.com/abstract=2339620

Gershon, R. A. (n.d.). Media Convergence. *Oxford Bibliographies*. Retrieved from http://www. oxfordbibliographies.com/view/document/obo-9780199756841/obo-9780199756841-0026.xml

Hinduja, S., & Patchin, J. W. (2010). Sexting: A brief guide to educators and parents. *Cyberbullying Research Center.* Retrieved from http://www.cyberbullying.us/Sexting_Fact_Sheet.pdf

Hinduja, S., & Patchin, J. W. (2013). Social influences on cyberbullying behaviors among middle and high school students. *Journal of Youth and Adolescence, 42*(5), 711-722. doi:10.1007/s10964-012-9902-4

Hoover, S. M., Clark, L. S., & Rainie, L. (2004). Faith online: 64% of wired Americans have used the Internet for spiritual or religious information. *Pew, Internet & American Life*. Retrieved from http://www.pewtrusts.org/en/about/news-room/press-releases/2004/04/07/64-of-online-americans-have-used-the-internet-for-spiritual-or-religious-purposes

Innis, H. A. (1949). *The press, a neglected factor in the economic history of the twentieth century*. London: Oxford University Press.

James, J. D. (1992). *Communicate on target: Vital keys for relationships and job success*. Singapore: AEF Publications.

Jenkins, H. (2006). *Fans, bloggers, and gamers: Exploring participatory culture*. New York: New York University Press.

Jenkins, H. (2008). The moral economy of Web 2.0 (Part two). *Aca-Fan*. Retrieved from http://henryjenkins.org/2008/03/the_moral_economy_of_web_20_pa_1.html#sthash.wHIQhBFs.dpuf

Jenkins, H. (2009). *Confronting the challenges of participatory culture: Media education for the 21st century*. Massachusetts: MIT Press.

Johnson, D. W., & Johnson, R. T. (1999). *Learning together and alone: Cooperative, competitive, and individualistic learning*. Needham Heights, MA: Allyn and Bacon.

MacManus, R. (2011). The future of the Internet is converged services. *Readwrite website*. Retrieved from http://readwrite.com/2011/08/28/the_future_of_the_internet_is_converged_services#awesm=~oHMGMzc7HsqTFP

Mehrabian, A. (1967). Orientation behaviors and nonverbal attitude communication. *Journal of Communication, 17*(4), 324-332. doi:10.1111/j.1460-2466.1967.tb01190.x

Mehrabian, A. (1971). *Silent Messages*. Belmont, CA:Wadsworth Publishing Company.

Palloff, R. M., & Pratt, K. (1999). *Building learning communities in cyberspace: Effective strategies for the online classroom*. San Francisco: Jossey-Bass.

Palme, J., & Berglund, M. (2002). *Anonymity on the Internet*. Retrieved from http://people.dsv.su.se/~jpalme/society/anonymity.html

Rovai, A. P. (2002). Development of an instrument to measure classroom community. *The Internet and Higher Education, 5*(3), 197-211. doi:10.1016/S1096-7516(02)00102-1

Rust, R. T., & Varki, S. (1996). Rising from the ashes of advertising. *Journal of Business Research, 37*(3), 173-181. doi:10.1016/S0148-2963(96)00067-7

Stahl, S. A., Hynd, C. R., Britton, B. K., McNish, & M. M., Bosquet, D. (1996). What happens when students read multiple source documents in history? *Clarke County School District*. Retrieved from http://curry.edschool.virginia.edu/go/clic/nrrc/hist_r45.html

Suler, J. (2004). The online disinhibition effect. *Cyberpsychology & Behaviour, 7*(3), 321-326. doi:10.1089/1094931041291295

Tillman, H. N. (2003). Evaluating quality on the Net. *Hope Tillman website*. Retrieved from http://www.hopetillman.com/findqual.html#

Toffler, A. (1980). *The third wave: The classic study of tomorrow*. New York, NY: Bantam.

Vaidhyanathan, S. (2011). *The Googlization of everything (and why we should worry)*. Berkely, CA: University of California Press.

Webster, C. (n.d.). *What is Cyberbullying?* Retrieved from http://www.cyberbullying.info/resources/downloads/ChrisWebster_WhatIsCyberbullying.pdf

Wegerif, R. (1998). The social dimension of asynchronous learning networks. *Journal of Asynchronous Learning Networks, 2*(1), 34-49.

World Bank. (2002). *Constructing knowledge societies: New challenges for tertiary education*. Washington: The World Bank. Retrieved from http://siteresources.worldbank.org/INTAFRREGTOPTEIA/Resources/Constructing_Knowledge_Societies.pdf

Ybarra, M., & Mitchell, K. J. (2004). Youth engaging in online harassment: Associations with caregiver-child relationships, Internet use, and personal characteristics. *Journal of Adolescence, 27*(3), 319-336. doi:10.1016/j.adolescence.2004.03.007

Websites

About.com Google website. (n.d.). Retrieved from http://google.about.com/od/googledesktop software/fr/earthrev.htm

Australian Institute of Criminology website. (2013). *Cybercrime*. Retrieved from http://www.aic.gov.au/crime_types/in_focus/cybercrime.html

BBC website. (n.d.). Retrieved from http://www.bbc.com/newsround/16612794

BusinessDictionary.com website. (n.d.). Retrieved from http://www.businessdictionary.com/definition/digital-media.html

European Union Internet report (1999). Working party on illegal and harmful content on the internet. *EC Report* [cited in Palme & Berglund, 2002].

Google Books website. (n.d.). Retrieved from http://books.google.com/googlebooks/library/

Google Scholar website. (n.d.). Retrieved from http://scholar.google.com.au/intl/en/scholar/about.html

Infosec Institute website. (2013). The impact of cybercrime. *Infosec Institute*. Retrieved from http://resources.infosecinstitute.com/2013-impact-cybercrime/

MDIA1001 website. (n.d.). Retrieved from http://www.unswbmedia.org/mdia1001/?p=3502

Mccrindle website. (2014). Retrieved from http://mccrindle.com.au/research-resources#infographics

Motherboard website. (2013). The best ways to visualize the Internet in real-time. *Motherboard*. Retrieved from http://motherboard.vice.com/en_uk/blog/the-best-ways-to-visualize-the-internet-in-real-time

News.com website. (2012). What is KONY 2012? Inside the campaign that stopped the world? *news.com.au*. Retrieved from http://www.news.com.au/world/its-all-over-the-webs-but-what-is-a-kony/story-e6frfkyi-1226292956990

Ofcom website. (2010). The communications market 2010: UK. *Ofcom*. Retrieved from http://www.ofcom.org.uk/static/cmr-10/UKCM-4.32.html

Online Services News website. (2013). Retrieved from https://mpreath.wordpress.com/category/news/

O'Reilly website. (n.d.). What is web 2.0? *O'Reilly*. Retrieved from http://oreilly.com/pub/a/web2/archive/what-is-web-20.html?page=2

PeaceWork website. (2006). Retrieved from http://www.peaceworkmagazine.org/print/51

The Linux Information Project website. (n.d.). *Internet definition.* Retrieved from http://www.linfo.org/internet.html

Webopedia website. (n.d.). Retrieved from http://www.webopedia.com/TERM/U/UGC.html

Webroot website. (2014). Internet pornography by the numbers; a significant threat to society. *Webroot*. Retrieved from http://www.webroot.com/au/en/home/resources/tips/digital-family-life/internet-pornography-by-the-numbers

Wikipedia website. (n.d.). *Instagram*. Retrieved from http://en.wikipedia.org/wiki/Instagram

Wikipedia website. (n.d.). *Google Earth*. Retrieved from http://en.wikipedia.org/wiki/Google_earth

1 Patterns of Internet usage in the Philippines[1]

Iremae D. Labucay[2]

Abstract

This chapter reports on the patterns of Internet use in the Philippines using survey data gathered by Social Weather Stations (SWS), a social research institute in the Philippines. As of March 2014, Internet usage rose to 35 percent of the population compared to 9 percent in 1998. However, the data indicates the presence of digital divide in Internet use with Internet use being higher in the capital city, in urban areas, among the middle-to-upper classes, college graduates and the youth. Filipino Internet users access the Internet largely for social networking rather than information seeking or learning, creativity and commercial activities, and entertainment and leisure.

Keywords: Internet use, Philippines, social networking, digital divide, Internet digital divide.

1.   Introduction

The first Filipino logged on to the Internet on March 29, 1994, when the Philippine Network Foundation obtained the country's first public permanent connection to the Internet (Minges, Magpantay, Firth, & Kelly, 2002). Since then, the number of Filipino Internet users has grown, gradually at first, but with

---

1. An earlier version of this chapter was presented as a paper at the Annual Conference of the World Association of Public Opinion Research (WAPOR) in Amsterdam, Netherlands, 2011. Prior to the conference, a draft version was written by the author in 2011 and is available on the web: http://wapor.org/wp-content/uploads/2011/09/Labucay.pdf. This chapter is based on the earlier papers but draws on updated research that was specifically done for this book project.

2. E-mail address: mae.labucay@sws.org.ph

How to cite this chapter: Labucay, I. D. (2014). Patterns of Internet usage in the Philippines. In J. D. James (Ed.), *The Internet and the Google age: Prospects and perils* (pp. 27-49). Dublin: Research-publishing.net. doi: 10.14705/rpnet.2014.000176

considerable rapidity in the last few years. The International Communication Union (ITU) estimates that the percentage of Filipino Internet users has grown from a mere 0.006 percent in 1998 to 36 percent in 2012 (World Bank, 2014). From these statistics, it is clear that Filipinos, indeed, are getting "sucked into [the] worldwide web" (Ho, 2009).

Yet despite this substantial growth of Internet use in the Philippines, there seems to be a scarcity of data on the Filipino Internet users' online behavior. The Yahoo!-Nielsen Net Index initiative, conducted since 2009, only gathers data on Internet users in National Urban Philippines in the 22 major cities across the country. In 2009, the Asia Institute of Journalism and Communication conducted for the United Nations Children's Fund (UNICEF) a nationwide survey on Internet access and use by Filipino schoolchildren. These studies, however, did not provide a comprehensive picture of the socio-demographic factors that promote (or hinder) access to and use of the Internet. Moreover, government-produced statistics on the usage of the Internet –or on information communication technology (ICT) for that matter– are limited, and do not separate the data by relevant socio-demographics. For instance, the Philippines does not have an entry on the official ITU table on percentage of Internet users, disaggregated by gender.

In this chapter, I aim to fill this research gap by presenting data from a series of nationally representative surveys on the patterns of Internet use among Filipino adults aged 18 and above. Using survey data gathered by SWS[1], a non-stock, non-profit, social research organization in the Philippines, I address these core questions:

- Who can access online?
- Who are online?
- How often do they go online?
- What do they do online?

---

1. Social Weather Stations (SWS) was established in August 1985 as a non-stock, non-profit, and non-partisan social research organization (www.sws.org.ph). Considered as Asia's oldest barometer, SWS has been generating survey-based national statistics on the quality of life, governance and public opinion in the Philippines.

In particular, I examine the socio-demographic differences that contribute to the digital divide in the Internet use and online activities of Filipinos. Digital divide, simply defined as the gap between the 'haves' and the 'have-nots', occurs at different levels: the "accessing divide" at the first level, and the "using divide" at the second level (Attewell, 2001; Cheong, 2007; Chinn & Fairlie, 2004; Norris, 2001; Zeng, 2011). *Accessing divide* refers to the gap in access and ownership of computers, by and large the most convenient way and, until recently, the only way to access the Internet. *Using divide*, on the other hand, refers to the gap that exists between/among the users themselves, particularly in the socio-demographic characteristics of the Internet users.

Previous research has shown that the patterns of access and use of the Internet vary across socio-demographic groups, and this would have a significant impact on how both the users and non-users could access the improved opportunities in education, employment and civic engagement brought on by the various aspects of the Internet (Norris, 2001; Ono & Zavodny, 2007). Moreover, socio-demographic characteristics have been found to be important predictors of a person's actions and behaviors (Ajzen & Fishbein, 1980, cited in Akman & Mishra, 2010, Zhang, 2005). I assume that knowing the trends in this gap between the Internet 'haves' and the 'have-nots' would enable policymakers to design initiatives specifically targeted at the 'have-nots'. In doing so, I also assume that bridging the digital divide is more pressing now that the benefits of the ICT and the Internet in human development and economic progress have been realized. In 1999, then UN Secretary General Kofi Annan considered the lack of access to ICT facilities as a deprivation as severe as the poor's lack of access to food, shelter and water:

> "People lack many things: jobs, shelter, food, health care, and drinkable water. Today, being cut off from basic telecommunications services is a hardship almost as acute as these other deprivations, and may indeed reduce the chances of finding remedies to them" (cited in Hassan, 2004, p. 67).

The UN initiative, *Millennium Development Goal* (MDG), identified in 2000 eight target areas for improvement in communications technology (UNICEF website, 2012). In 2011, the United Nations Special Rapporteur on the promotion and protection of the right to freedom of opinion and expression submitted a report to the UN Human Rights Council, making several recommendations to promote and protect the "right to freedom of expression online". And since 2001, the World Economic Forum's Global Information Technology Report and the Networked Readiness Index (NRI) have been providing an update on the current state of ICT readiness of countries as a means to foster economic growth and competitiveness.

2.   Methods

2.1.   Data source

As mentioned above, the main data source for this chapter is survey data on Internet access and Internet use gathered by SWS from 1997 to 2014 through its quarterly Social Weather Surveys. Data were gathered through face-to-face interviews of a nationally representative sample of 1,200 voting age adults (18 years old and above) per quarter. The Philippines was divided into four major study areas: Metro Manila, Balance Luzon (areas outside of Metro Manila but within Luzon), Visayas and Mindanao. The sample size was equally divided into 300 respondents in each of the four study areas (sampling error margins of ±3.0 percent for national percentages, ±6.0 percent for each of the four study areas). Multi-stage probability sampling was used in selecting the adult respondents.

2.2.   Measures

Starting in March 2011, Internet use was explored by simply asking "Do you ever go online to access the Internet or the World Wide Web or send and receive email?". Then, a follow-up question was asked to determine frequency of use, with the respondents choosing from six response categories: "a few times a day", "at least once a day", "3-5 days a week", "1-2 days a week", "every other week", and "less often". To simplify reporting, however, these seven response categories were reduced to three categories: *frequent* (at least daily), *moderate* (at least weekly), and *infrequent* (less than weekly).

Social Weather Surveys also regularly obtain information and background characteristics of the respondents, such as gender, age, locale, educational attainment, marital status, work status, and household facilities. Socio-economic class was used as a proxy indicator of household income. Socio-economic classification, which is often used in market research, divides the population into four categories: the rich classes (AB), the middle class (C), the poor (D), and the very poor (E). Based on our standard SWS practice, the rich and the middle classes are combined as middle-to-upper classes (ABC). Unless otherwise specified, the annual data is presented as averages from the quarterly surveys.

3.   Findings

3.1.   Who can access online?

SWS data on household facilities from 1997 through 2013 shows that computer ownership in the Filipino household was generally low and hardly changed until 2008 when it reached double-digit levels. Data on computer ownership is an important measure of Internet use because computers have long been the only device needed to access the Internet.

The ownership of computers in the household has ranged from 3 percent in 1997 to 7 percent in 2007, before it increased to 10 percent in 2008. Sixteen percent of households in both 2012 and 2013 had computers at home. In absolute terms, the proportion of households with computers increased from 414,000 in 1997 (out of the projected 12.8 million households) to 3.8 million in 2013 (out of the projected 21.5 million households).

Computer penetration in the household has always been the highest in Metro Manila, in urban areas, and among middle-to-upper classes (ABC). Computer ownership in the provincial areas, in rural localities and among classes D and E have considerably increased since 1997, but ownership among these demographics remains disproportionately lower.

As of 2013, households in Metro Manila were at least twice more likely than households in the provincial areas to own a computer. By locale, computer ownership was three times higher in urban households than in rural households. The disparity in access to computers was more noticeable across socio-economic classes: 53 percent of households in classes ABC owned a computer, twice the *combined* percentage of households in classes D and E who owned a computer.

Table 1.   Internet access in the household, Philippines, 1998 through 2013: percent of households with Internet connection[1]

	'98	'99	'00	'01	'02	'03	'04	'05	'06	'07	'08	'09	'10	'11	'12	'13
Total Philippines	2	1	2	2	3	3	2	2	2	2	4	4	6	7	8	9
Area																
Metro Manila	9	8	11	12	14	18	10	7	7	7	11	11	14	17	18	19
Balance Luzon	0	0	0	0	2	2	1	2	1	2	4	5	7	6	7	9
Visayas	0	1	1	1	1	1	1	1	2	2	3	3	6	8	10	7
Mindanao	0	0	0	0	1	0	0	1	2	1	1	1	2	2	3	5
Locale																
Urban	3	2	4	5	6	7	5	4	3	4	7	8	10	11	12	14
Rural	0	0	0	0	0	0	0	0	1	1	1	1	2	2	3	3
Socio-economic Class																
Classes ABC	13	12	18	21	24	29	10	10	10	13	19	21	29	27	26	38
Class D	0	0	0	0	1	1	2	2	2	2	4	5	6	7	9	10
Class E	0	0	0	0	0	0	0	0	0	0	0	1	1	0	2	1

Table 1 above shows that access to Internet in the household is even lower than computer ownership. The percentages of households with computers with

1. Source: Data from Social Weather Stations, Philippines, 1997 through 2013.

Internet connection have ranged between 1 percent to 4 percent from 1997 through 2009, before it slightly increased to 6 percent in 2010, 7 percent in 2011, 8 percent in 2012 and 9 percent in 2013. These correspond to an increase from 230,000 households with Internet access in 1998 (out of the projected 14.4 million households) to 2.2 million households with Internet access in 2010 (out of the projected 21.5 million households).

From 1998 to 2013, households with Internet connection in Metro Manila have ranged from 7 percent to 19 percent. In provincial areas, however, Internet penetration remains well below 10 percent. Internet penetration in urban households gradually increased from 3 percent in 1998 to 14 percent in 2010, but in the rural areas, Internet access was zero until the 1 percent mark was reached in 2006. By socio-economic class, Internet penetration is now 38 percent among ABC class households, in contrast to households in class D, where it is 10 percent at its highest in 2013, and in class E, where Internet penetration was zero until 2008.

3.2.   Who are online?

As of March 2014, about one in three (32 percent) Filipino adults goes online to access the Internet or send and receive emails. This is equivalent to 19.4 million people out of the projected 59.8 million of the adult population in the nation.

The percentage of Internet users ranged from 9 percent to 12 percent between 2006 and 2009, then slightly increased to 16 percent in 2009 and 17 percent in 2011 before it doubled to 25 percent in 2012 and to 26 percent in 2013, before reaching the all-time high of 32 percent in 2014.

Table 2 shows the socio-demographic characteristics of adult Filipino Internet users from 2006 to 2014. Internet use remains highest in Metro Manila, in urban areas, among middle-to-upper classes ABC, youth aged between 18-24, and college graduates. Whereas Internet use has increased in the other demographic groups since 2006, the Internet digital divide still remains (more on this below).

Table 2.   Demographics of Filipino Internet users, Philippines, averages per Year, 2006 – 2013[1]

	2006	2007	2008	2009	2010	2011	2012	2013	2014
Total Philippines	9	11	11	12	16	17	25	26	32
Area									
NCR	16	22	23	23	27	31	38	42	38
Balance Luzon	6	11	11	14	15	16	27	26	36
Visayas	14	9	9	10	16	15	22	28	29
Mindanao	8	5	6	6	10	10	17	16	24
Locale									
Urban	13	17	17	19	22	24	35	35	41
Rural	5	3	4	6	8	9	16	15	22
Socio-economic Class									
Classes ABC	16	25	26	31	30	38	51	49	66
Class D	10	12	13	14	17	18	28	28	35
Class E	6	4	4	6	8	6	11	13	18
Sex									
Men	10	12	12	13	16	17	25	26	34
Women	9	9	11	12	15	16	26	26	31
Age group									
18-24	27	26	32	35	47	44	58	62	74
25-34	11	13	16	15	21	22	35	37	45
35-44	8	10	7	11	14	14	23	24	37
45-54	4	3	6	5	5	9	16	15	13
55 and above	2	4	2	3	3	4	8	7	8
Educational Attainment									
No formal education/ Some elementary	1	0	0	1	1	1	1	3	6
Up to elementary graduate	2	3	2	3	4	5	9	10	14
Up to high school graduate	12	13	14	16	21	23	34	34	44
College graduate/Post-college	34	35	34	36	45	46	65	56	60
Civil Status									
Married/With Live-in Partner	7	8	7	9	11	13	21	21	28
Unmarried	21	22	20	21	26	34	38	42	46

1. Source: Data from Social Weather Stations, Philippines, 2006 to 2014.

Question wording from 2011 onwards was "Do you ever go online to access the internet or the World Wide Web or send and receive email?"; Question wording from 2006 to 2010 was "Do you use a computer at your workplace, at school, at home, or anywhere else at least on an occasional basis? IF YES, Do you ever go online to access the internet or the World Wide Web or send and receive email?"

The year 2013 includes registered voters.

	2006	2007	2008	2009	2010	2011	2012	2013	2014
Work Status									
Working	12	13	12	13	16	17	24	23	33
Not working	8	10	9	11	15	22	26	30	31
Presence of Overseas Filipino Worker (OFW) in the Household									
With OFW in the Household	--	--	--	--	--	--	42	45	57
Without OFW in the Household	--	--	--	--	--	--	22	24	31

In 2014, the gap in Internet use in Metro Manila and the provincial areas has considerably narrowed down, as the percentage of Internet users reached all-time high levels in Balance Luzon (36 percent), Visayas (29 percent) and Mindanao (24 percent). Nevertheless, the Internet use gap remains higher in Metro Manila than in the provincial areas. By locale, the Internet use gap between urban and rural dwellers remains. About two-fifths (41 percent) of urban dwellers in 2014 are Internet users, about twice more than the 22 percent among rural dwellers.

In 2014, three-fifths (66 percent) of *middle-to-upper* classes ABC are Internet users, nearly twice more than *poor* class D (35 percent) and three times more than those from the *very poor* class E (18 percent) who are also Internet users. In the first quarter of 2014, Internet use among lower classes D and E reached all-time high levels, but the increase was offset by the corresponding increase among classes ABC. Internet use among classes ABC reached 25-26 percent level in 2007-2008, when it was only 12-13 percent among class D and 4 percent among class E. The rate of Internet adoption is higher among class D than class E.

Men and women are equally likely to use the Internet. In 2014, there are about one-third of both men and women who are Internet users, an increase from one-fourth in both 2012 and 2013.

Age is a strong predictor of Internet use, such that Internet use is highest among the youth and it decreases with age. Three-fourths of the intermediate youth aged 18-24 are Internet users, compared to only 13 percent among those aged 45-54 and 8 percent among those aged 55 and above. Internet adoption rates reached an all-time high among those 25-34 and 35-44, but it hardly changed across time among those aged 45 and above. Among the 25-34, it increased from one-third in 2012-2013 to 45 percent in 2014, and among the 35-44, it increased from about one-fourth in 2012-2013 to 37 percent in 2014.

Internet use increases with education. In 2014, about three-fifths of college graduates are Internet users, compared to only about a tenth of those with elementary education or less. Internet usage has always been higher among college graduates than those with less education.

From 2006 to 2011, Internet usage among college graduates was about two times more than the combined Internet usage among those from the lower three levels of education: high school graduates, elementary graduates and non-elementary graduates. The gap has narrowed down in 2012 and 2013, especially between the college graduates and the high school graduates. Nonetheless, the rate of Internet adoption among those with less education remains far lower than college graduates.

Since 2006, Internet use has always been higher among the unmarried people than those who are married or who have live-in partners. As many as one-third of unmarried adults are Internet users, nearly three times more than the percentage of married people who use the Internet.

Work status is hardly a factor in Internet use, as Internet usage is about the same among working adults and non-working adults. In 2011, however, occupation types among those working was found to be a strong indicator of Internet use, with Internet use higher among the hired workers (particularly among the managers, professionals/technical workers, and those involved in clerical/ administrative/sales) than the employers and self-employed.

One important finding is that the presence of an Overseas Filipino Worker (OFW) in the household has a significant impact on Internet use. The Philippines is the second-largest labor-exporting country after Mexico, with 4.7 million Filipinos working in about 197 countries around the world (Guerrero, Labucay, Sandoval,

& Mangahas, 2009). In 2014, one in two of those with OFW in their households is an Internet user. From 2012 to 2014, Internet usage rate is twice as high among those with OFWs in the household compared to those without.

Internet use is higher among those who have access to computer and Internet connection in the household. Three-fifths of adults with computers in the household are Internet users, compared to only one-fourth of those without computers. As many as three-fourths of those with computers with Internet connection at home are Internet users, compared to only about one-fifth of those without Internet connection at home.

3.2.1. Internet use by proxy

Despite the low percentage of Internet use among adult Filipinos, a large majority of the non-Internet users are, in fact, 'proxy users'. Proxy Internet users are defined in Dutton, Helsper and Gerber (2009) as those "who use the Internet through another person, such as a family member, but who do not use it themselves in a more direct way" (p. 17). Seventy percent of non-Internet users say they know of someone who could access the Internet on their behalf. Non-users are mostly likely to ask their friends and children/grandchildren to access the Internet on their behalf.

As shown in Table 3, the demographics (particularly class and educational attainment) of proxy Internet users closely resemble the demographics of Internet users. By area, proxy Internet use is about four-fifths in Metro Manila and Balance Luzon and about three-fifths in Visayas, compared to about two-fifths in Mindanao. Four-fifths of classes ABC and 70 percent of class D are proxy Internet users, compared to 64 percent among class E. Proxy Internet use increases with education: about four-fifths among college graduates, compared to 50 percent among non-elementary graduates.

In contrast, proxy Internet use is highest among the oldest age group. Nearly all of those aged 45 and above are proxy Internet users, compared to only 47 percent among the 18-24 age group.

Table 3. Demographics of proxy Internet users, Philippines: percent of non-Internet users who could ask other people to use the Internet for them[1] – (% of each group of Filipino adults 18 and above who do not use the Internet)

	Proxy Internet Users (%)
Total Philippines	70
Area	
Metro Manila	80
Balance Luzon	76
Visayas	69
Mindanao	35
Locale	
Urban	70
Rural	69
Socio-economic class	
Classes ABC	80
Class D	70
Class E	64
Gender	
Men	67
Women	74
Age	
18-24	47
25-34	67
35-44	74
45-54	95
55 and above	95
Educational Attainment	
No formal education/Some elementary	50
Up to elementary graduate	75
Up to high school graduate	62
College graduate/Post-college	83

1. Source: Data from Social Weather Stations, Philippines, 2011.

Question wording: "If you need to use the Internet to send/receive an email or do something using the Internet, do you know someone who could access the Internet and do this for you? And who could you ask for help in accessing for you? (SHOWCARD) (ALLOW MULTIPLE RESPONSE)".

3.3. How often do they go online?

About half to three-fifths of Internet users are *frequent* to *moderate* users, while one-third are *infrequent* users (less than once per week). Frequent users are those who use the Internet at least once daily, while moderate users are those who use it at least once a week. Across time, the percentage of frequent to moderate users hardly varied.

Internet users from Metro Manila, urban areas, classes ABC and who are college graduates use the Internet more frequently than the other groups. As high as half of Internet users in Metro Manila and about two-fifths in Balance Luzon are frequent Internet users. By class, as high as 58 percent of classes ABC are frequent Internet users, compared to only about two-fifths among class D. Frequency of Internet use hardly varies by age. Nevertheless, in 2011 and in 2014, about half of those 55 and above are frequent Internet users, higher than the younger age groups.

The percentage of frequent Internet users has always been higher among college graduates than those with less education. About two-fifths of the college graduates are daily Internet users, compared to about one-fifth to one-third among those with less education.

Two-fifths of the college graduates are frequent users, compared to about one-fourth of the less educated who are also daily users. About half of Internet users in households who own computers and 54 percent of those in households with Internet connection are also frequent users.

3.4. What do they do online?

The surveys tested for nine Internet activities that are classified into five broad categories based on the typology used by the Internet in a Britain report are:

- *social networking* (online social networking like Facebook, Twitter);
- *information seeking or learning* (to access news, get health information, etc.);

- *creativity and production* (blogging, share own photos, videos and stories);
- *entertainment and leisure* (play online games);
- *commercial activity* (online purchasing).

Social networking is by far the single most popular online activity among Filipino Internet users, with as many as 95 percent who access online social networking sites such as Facebook (or Friendster), although Twitter is only used by about two-fifths of the Internet users. The least popular online activities are blogging and online shopping, with less than a tenth of Internet users utilizing either of these. Social networking is followed in a distant second by about half who share online (presumably through social networks) things that they have created themselves, such as their own artwork, photos, stories or videos.

Of the three *information seeking or learning* activities tested, the most common ones are: getting news on current events and searching for information on health, dieting and fitness. There are slightly fewer users who search for sensitive health information or health topics that are difficult to talk about, like drug use, sexual health and depression. As shown in Table 4, Table 5, and Table 6, there are mixed socio-demographic patterns on the online activities of Filipino Internet users.

3.4.1. Social networking

Online social networking is dominant across socio-demographic groups, but is noticeably higher among those aged 18 to 34 than those aged 35 and above. Use of social media is also higher amongst those with at least an elementary education than those who did not graduate from elementary school. Across the period 2011 through 2014, use of online social networking has increased from about 80 percent to more than 90 percent in Visayas and Mindanao and among class E.

Twitter use is only slightly more popular in Metro Manila than in the other large cities, especially among the 18-34 age group and college graduates.

Table 4. Internet Activities: Online social networking,
by socio-demographic characteristics,
2011 through 2014[1]

	Online social networking like Facebook					Use Twitter			
	2011	2012	2013	2014		2011	2012	2013	2014
Total Philippines	89	87	89	95		15	19	14	19
Area									
Metro Manila	86	93	93	93		20	19	24	20
Balance Luzon	93	86	89	95		12	23	13	21
Visayas	85	82	88	93		12	13	11	13
Mindanao	86	86	85	99		24	17	8	18
Locale									
Urban	93	89	90	95		15	19	15	23
Rural	78	84	88	95		17	21	12	11
Socio-economic class									
Classes ABC	91	76	88	94		21	21	18	6
Class D	89	90	90	95		15	20	14	20
Class E	91	86	84	96		8	11	12	20
Gender									
Men	88	87	87	94		16	25	14	22
Women	91	87	91	96		14	14	14	16
Age									
18-24	93	97	93	96		18	26	18	22
25-34	87	85	94	98		18	23	16	19
35-44	90	81	87	95		13	12	10	18
45-54	75	83	69	88		0	10	9	13
55 and above	100	78	72	86		17	10	13	17
Educational Attainment									
No formal education/ Some elementary	73	84	18	100		0	26	0	16
Up to elementary graduate	89	83	88	95		21	18	4	12
Up to high school graduate	90	90	91	94		13	20	14	17
College graduate/ Post-college	89	82	87	98		18	18	19	29

1. Question wording: "We're interested in the kinds of things you do on the Internet. Please just tell me whether you ever do each activity in the Internet, or not. Do you ever... [MENTION ACTIVITY]? (SHUFFLE CARDS)" [Use an online social networking sites like Facebook or Friendster, Use Twitter].

Table 5.   Internet Activities: Information seeking/learning,
           by socio-demographic characteristics, 2011 through 2014[1]

	Current Events or Politics				Health, Dieting and Fitness				Sensitive Health information			
	2011	2012	2013	2014	2011	2012	2013	2014	2012	2013	2014	2014
Total Philippines	40	41	33	46	37	31	43	47	28	24	30	29
Area												
Metro Manila	41	40	37	54	49	33	49	50	33	27	35	36
Balance Luzon	36	41	36	47	37	28	51	50	32	25	33	30
Visayas	30	43	23	48	28	34	26	48	18	16	22	37
Mindanao	62	43	28	33	30	38	28	32	19	21	19	12
Locale												
Urban	41	40	36	49	38	32	47	49	30	23	32	30
Rural	37	44	23	39	35	29	33	42	21	25	24	27
Socio-economic class												
Classes ABC	51	37	37	57	48	39	61	63	42	20	44	63
Class D	39	43	33	45	37	30	43	48	28	26	29	28
Class E	29	38	23	45	24	23	24	29	6	15	20	17
Gender												
Men	36	46	36	51	33	29	42	43	24	22	25	32
Women	43	38	29	40	42	33	44	50	32	25	34	·26
Age												
18-24	43	43	34	40	37	21	41	40	29	25	32	28
25-34	33	41	33	54	38	30	45	48	21	23	28	26
35-44	52	35	32	39	47	54	43	50	44	22	31	33
45-54	21	49	24	46	22	39	48	44	16	31	28	28
55 and above	70	42	33	56	30	12	43	57	30	13	33	36
Educational Attainment												
No formal education	0	26	0	31	0	68	0	19	0	42	0	0
Up to elementary graduate	33	29	9	32	36	9	13	24	21	9	4	17
Up to high school graduate	37	40	30	47	37	28	42	46	26	22	29	29
College graduate/ Post-college	49	49	47	52	40	42	57	62	35	30	41	39

1. Note. Question wording: "We're interested in the kinds of things you do on the Internet. Please just tell me whether you ever do each activity in the Internet, or not. Do you ever... [MENTION ACTIVITY]? (SHUFFLE CARDS)" [Go online or to the Internet to get news or information about current events or politics, Look online or in the Internet for information on health, dieting, or physical fitness, Look for information online or in the Internet about a health topic that's hard to talk about, like drug use, sexual health, or depression].

Table 6. Internet Activities: Creative activities,
by socio-demographic characteristics, 2011 through 2014[1]

	Share something you created online				Create or work on own blog			
	2011	2012	2013	2014	2012	2013	2014	2014
Total Philippines	44	38	50	51	5	8	4	6
Area								
Metro Manila	51	41	60	57	10	10	5	6
Balance Luzon	46	40	51	51	2	11	4	7
Visayas	35	32	45	53	7	2	1	7
Mindanao	38	31	34	40	5	2	4	1
Locale								
Urban	44	37	49	49	4	9	4	8
Rural	42	39	51	53	8	7	2	1
Socio-economic class								
Classes ABC	59	32	51	72	8	9	7	5
Class D	42	41	50	49	5	9	3	5
Class E	37	26	44	46	4	2	4	14
Gender								
Men	48	39	48	51	6	7	5	6
Women	38	36	51	50	4	10	3	6
Age								
18-24	46	45	55	59	5	4	4	6
25-34	35	43	50	52	8	13	5	8
35-44	57	33	47	45	4	9	3	3
45-54	39	29	36	50	0	7	0	3
55 and above	30	5	43	33	0	0	6	12
Educational Attainment								
No formal education/Some elementary	51	26	0	44	0	0	0	10
Up to elementary graduate	52	31	49	46	7	13	4	5
Up to high school graduate	36	40	51	49	5	8	4	6
College graduate/ Post-college	54	36	49	58	5	8	5	6

1. Question wording: "We're interested in the kinds of things you do on the Internet. Please just tell me whether you ever do each activity in the Internet, or not. Do you ever... [MENTION ACTIVITY]? (SHUFFLE CARDS)" [Share something online that you created yourself, such as your own artwork, photos, stories or videos; Create or work on your own online journal or blog.

3.4.2.   Information seeking/learning

In all three information seeking/learning online activities, class and education appears to be an important predictor of usage, to the extent that use of the Internet for news or health information increases the higher the class and educational attainment of the Internet users.

Using the Internet to access news articles is slightly more popular among Internet users from classes ABC and D, those aged 55 and above and college graduates.

Searching for health information, on the other hand, is more popular in Metro Manila and Balance Luzon, among classes ABC, among the 35-44 age group and college graduates.

Searching for sensitive health information, meanwhile, is more popular in Metro Manila and Balance Luzon, among classes ABC, and college graduates.

3.4.3.   Creativity and production

Sharing online blogs and photos that individuals created themselves is a popular Internet activity in Metro Manila and Balance Luzon, amongst classes ABC, those aged 18-45, and those with some elementary education or higher.

Blogging activity is low and hardly varies across all demographics.

3.4.4.   Entertainment and leisure

Playing online games is more popular among Internet users in Metro Manila, Visayas and Mindanao than in Balance Luzon. Online games are also more popular among Internet users classes D and E, who are males, aged 18-34, and who have some elementary education or higher.

Online purchasing, like blogging, is low and hardly varies across all demographics.

4.   Discussion

In this chapter I have outlined the patterns of Internet use in the Philippines using data gathered from various nationally representative surveys. Survey data show that while the percentage remains low compared to developed countries, Internet use has grown considerably in the nation over the last few years. Access to computers and Internet connection in the household has also started to increase. Yet the findings indicate that the Philippines is experiencing a 'digital divide', and because of this, the barriers to overcome Internet connectivity and use need to be urgently addressed.

Survey data from the Philippines is in keeping with previous findings which showed that households in the provincial areas, rural localities, and those who belong to lower socio-economic classes are less likely to own a computer and have Internet connection at home than households from the capital city, urban areas and upper-to-middle classes (see Attewell, 2001; Chinn & Fairlie, 2004; Norris, 2001).

Results from the Philippines, to some extent, correspond with previous findings on the variations in Internet use across socio-demographic groups. One finding specifically related to the Philippines' socio-economic setting is that the adults in households with family members who are working overseas are twice more likely to use the Internet than those without an overseas worker in the household. For the families left in the country, the Internet has become a convenient and efficient means of communicating with their family members abroad. Indeed, it is now easier to communicate with people using Internet applications such as web chats, online video calls, or even posting photos and pictures through Facebook.

Internet use is higher in the Metro Manila area than in provincial areas and the same applies in urban areas compared to rural areas, confirming Gardner and Oswald's (2001) findings of a north/south divide in Internet use. Internet use is also higher among those from upper-to-middle classes ABC than those from lower classes D and E, and the more educated (see Choi, 2008; Gardner &

Oswald, 2001; Howard, Rainie, & Jones, 2002; Norris, 2001; Smith et al., 2008). Internet users from classes ABC are also more likely to use the Internet more frequently than those from classes D and E.

Filipino men and women are equally likely to use the Internet, supporting the findings of Jackson, Ervin, Gardner, and Schmitt (2001) and Smith et al. (2008)[1].

Youth are the key drivers of Internet use in the Philippines in the sense that while about three in four of those aged 18-24 are Internet users, only about a tenth of those aged 55 and above are Internet users. This pattern clearly validates the stereotype that younger individuals are greater Internet users than the older individuals (see Chinn & Fairlie, 2004; Choi, 2008; Gardner & Oswald, 2001; Howard et al., 2002; Norris, 2001; Smith et al., 2008).

While Internet use among adult Filipinos is still low compared with other countries, survey data also indicates that the majority of non-users are proxy Internet users who could ask their family members and their friends to access the Internet on their behalf. The demographics of proxy Internet users are similar to those of actual Internet users, however, this could further widen the gap in Internet use between those from the capital city or near the capital city, and those from classes ABC and D and E. Notably, almost all of the older age groups 45 and above are proxy Internet users.

As to the patterns of what Filipino Internet users do online, online social networking is largely the most popular online activity, and its usage hardly varies across socio-demographic groups. To some extent, Philippines' results are consistent with previous research that younger Internet users tend to do more fun activities such as online social networking, playing online games while older people do more information seeking/learning activities, particularly viewing news on current events (see Howard et al., 2002; Madden & Rainie, 2003). The

1. It should be noted, however, that other studies show contradictory findings, reporting higher Internet use among men than women (see Bimber, 2000; Choi, 2008; Gardner & Oswald, 2001; Howard et al., 2002; Norris, 2001; Ono & Zavodny, 2003). Nevertheless, it has also been predicted that the gender divide in Internet use is likely to narrow as the educational and income status of women improve.

more educated classes and those from higher socio-economic classes also tend to go online to access news and health information.

5.   Conclusion

This chapter contributes to a greater understanding of the current trends in Internet use among Filipinos nationwide. By showing that there are differences in Internet use and access across socio-demographic groups nationwide, it is hoped that the data presented would be considered in the efforts of the government and private sector to bridge the digital divide by focusing on those who do not have access to or do not use the Internet; those in the provinces, the rural areas, the poor and lower income individuals. It should be noted that increasing the percentage of Internet users is part of the MDG indicators, and that the government, therefore, should not only focus on addressing the MDG indicators related to hunger and poverty. After all, as noted by Kofi Annan, the lack of access to Internet is also a deprivation.

Moreover, the trends in Internet use should also be understood within the context of improving the interconnectedness of the various stakeholders of the Philippines' economy. In the 2014 Networked Readiness Index, the Philippines improved its ranking to become slightly higher than the average of the lower-middle-income countries. Nevertheless, the Philippines still lags behind Singapore, Malaysia and Thailand, and is only slightly higher than Vietnam.

Bridging the Internet divide is imperative for the government if it wants to further bolster the competitiveness of the Philippines' economy, particularly by 2015 when the ASEAN Economic Community will be launched. While Internet adoption rate in the Philippines is higher than the other developing countries, like Myanmar (1 percent), Cambodia (5 percent), Laos (11 percent), Indonesia (15 percent), and Thailand (26 percent), it is comparably lower than the Internet adoption rates in Malaysia (66 percent) and Singapore (74 percent).

It is hoped that further research on Filipino Internet users can be undertaken, especially with regard to the social impact of the Internet, particularly online social networking.

References

Ajzen, I., & Fishbein, M. (1980). Understanding attitudes and predicting social behavior. Englewood Cliffs, NJ: PrenticeHall, Inc.

Akman, I., & Mishra, A. (2010). Gender, age and income differences in Internet usage among employees in organizations. *Computers in Human Behavior, 26*(3), 482-490. doi:10.1016/j.chb.2009.12.007

Attewell, P. (2001). The first and second digital divides. *Sociology of Education, 74*(3), 252-259. doi:10.2307/2673277

Bimber, B. (2000). Measuring the gender gap on the Internet. *Social Science Quarterly, 81*(3), 868-876.

Cheong, P. H. (2007). Gender and perceived Internet efficacy: Examining secondary digital divide issues in Singapore. *Women's Studies in Communication, 30*(2), 205-228. doi:10.1 080/07491409.2007.10162513

Chinn, M. D., & Fairlie, R. (2004). The determinants of the global digital divide: A cross-country analysis of computer and Internet penetration. *Oxford Economic Papers, 59*(1). doi:10.3386/w10686

Choi, A. (2008). Internet in Singapore: Findings from a national survey. *Observatorio (OBS) Journal, 6*, 151-168.

Dutton, W. H., Helsper, E. J., & Gerber, M. M. (2009). *The Internet in Britain: 2009*. Oxford: Oxford Internet Institute.

Gardner, J., & Oswald, A. (2001). *Internet use: The digital divide*. Retrieved from www2. warwick.ac.uk/fac/soc/economics/staff/faculty/oswald/bsago12.pdf

Guerrero, L. L. B., Labucay, I. D., Sandoval, G. A., & Mangahas, M. (2009). Where's a Great Place to Work: A Global Analysis from the Perspective of a Labor-Exporting Country. In M. Haller, R. Jowell, & T. W. Smith (Eds), *The international social survey programme 1984-2009: Charting the globe*. Oxon: Routledge.

Hassan, R. (2004). *Media, politics and the network society*. Berkshire, England: McGraw-Hill.

Ho, A. L. (2009, December 04). Filipinos get sucked into worldwide web. *Philippine Daily Inquirer*. Retrieved from http://technology.inquirer.net/infotech/infotech/view/20090412-198910/Filipinos-get-sucked-into-worldwide-web

Howard, P. E. N., Rainie, L., & Jones, S. (2002). Days and nights on the Internet. In B. Wellman & C. Haythornthwaite (Eds), *The Internet in everyday life*. Oxford: Blackwell Publishing.

Jackson, L. A., Ervin, K. S., Gardner, P. D., & Schmitt, N. (2001). Gender and the Internet: Women communicating and men searching. *Sex Roles, 44*(5), 363-379. doi:10.1023/A:1010937901821

Madden, M., & Rainie, L. (2003). America's online pursuits: The changing picture of who's online and what they do. *Pew Internet & American Life Project*. Retrieved from http://www.pewinternet.org/files/old-media/Files/Reports/2003/PIP_Online_Pursuits_Final.PDF.PDF

Minges, M., Magpantay, E., Firth, L., & Kelly, T. (2002). *Pinoy Internet: Philippines case study*. Geneva, Switzerland: International Telecommunication Union's (ITU). Retrieved from https://www.itu.int/asean2001/reports/material/PHL%20CS.pdf

Norris, P. (2001). *Digital divide: Civic engagement, information poverty, and the Internet worldwide*. Cambridge: Cambridge University Press. doi:10.1017/CBO9781139164887

Ono, H., & Zavodny, M. (2003). Gender and the Internet. *Social Science Quarterly, 84*(1), 111-121. doi:10.1111/1540-6237.t01-1-8401007

Ono, H., & Zavodny, M. (2007). Digital inequality: A five country comparison using microdata. *Social Science Research, 36*(3), 1135-1155. doi:10.1016/j.ssresearch.2006.09.001

Smith, P., Smith, N., Sherman, K., Kriplani, K., Goodwin, I., Bell, A., & Crothers, C. (2008). The Internet: Social and demographic impacts in Aotearoa New Zealand. *Observatorio (OBS) Journal*. 307-330.

Unicef website. (2012). Millenium development goals (MDG) monitoring. *Unicef Statistics and Monitoring*. Retrieved from http://www.unicef.org/statistics/index_24304.html

World Bank. (2014). World development indicators 2014. Washington, DC: World Bank. doi:10.1596/978-1-4648-0163-1

Zeng, F. (2011). College students perception of the second-level digital divide: An empirical analysis. *Asian Social Science, 7*(6), 42-50. doi:10.5539/ass.v7n6p42

Zhang, Y. (2005). Age, gender, and Internet attitudes among employees in the business world. *Computers in Human Behavior, 21*(1), 1-10. doi:10.1016/j.chb.2004.02.006

2 The gendered search to connect: Females and social media in rural, Northern Ireland

Anne Rice[1]

Abstract

Technology has changed family life and nowadays most of us live in 'virtual homes' from which we can connect with anyone, anywhere. This has the potential to improve the quality of social capital between geographically separated family members. Social capital refers to the relationships individuals form with each other and the resources obtained from these relationships (Coleman, 1988; Halpern, 2005). It is a concept that differentiates between bridging (weak ties that provide information) and bonding (strong bonds that provide emotional support) social capital (Putnam, 2000). This chapter reveals that social networking websites such as Facebook help maintain connections between family at home and those that have emigrated. As such, a new level of global family social capital (Rice, 2014) has emerged in the social networking era. However, for rural families it is often the case that mothers are at the center of global family social capital and fathers remain on the margins. This chapter outlines the under-representation of rural fathers in terms of social networking use and discusses what impact this has on them as individuals and more widely on established social capital theory.

Keywords: social capital, Facebook in Ireland, gender and the Internet, social media and rural communities.

1. E-mail address: arice05@qub.ac.uk

How to cite this chapter: Rice, A. (2014). The gendered search to connect: Females and social media in rural, Northern Ireland. In J. D. James (Ed.), *The Internet and the Google age: Prospects and perils* (pp. 51-61). Dublin: Research-publishing.net. doi:10.14705/rpnet.2014.000177

1. Introduction

As the use of the Internet increases, more and more people are using technologies and social networking websites such as Facebook, Twitter and LinkedIn. Social networking sites have been defined by Boyd and Ellison (2007) as "web-based services that allow individuals to (1) construct a public or semi public profile within a bounded system; (2) articulate a list of other users with whom they share a connection; and (3) view and traverse their list of connections and those made by others within the system" (p. 221). The use of these sites has been accompanied by, and contributed to, significant shifts in social interaction. For example, today, individual family members frequently exchange messages from their computers and phones to loved ones on the other side of the world. From the comfort of their own home, families can stay connected with people geographically separated from them. The scale of this change to modern family relations is massive with 1.3 billion people worldwide now using Facebook (Albergotti, 2014). However, little is known about which family members take responsibility for nurturing online connections with those separated from them by emigration. This study hopes to fill the research gap in this area.

This chapter is based on research carried out between 2010 and 2011 in a rural area of Northern Ireland. It involved 11 focus groups and 36 in-depth interviews with young people (aged 16-18) and their parents. The research examined the impact of the social networking website, Facebook, on individual, community and family social capital. Based on findings from this investigation, the chapter specifically examines the outcome of Facebook use for family social capital. It reveals gender differences in terms of who is searching to stay connected in the new era of global family social capital.

The chapter begins with an overview of the female investment in global family social capital (Rice, 2014). It then progresses to discuss the lack of interest by fathers in regard to social networking in rural areas. The chapter then acknowledges the limitations of this study. Finally, the implications of these findings are discussed –how they impact traditional social capital theory and rural males.

2. Female investment in global family social capital

Traditionally, family social capital was mostly found in the relationships between family members who were bound together in shared physical locations (Coleman, 1988). Nowadays, the Internet has facilitated the spread of social capital across geographical boundaries. Unlike previous generations, family members can invest in global family social capital. However, in this study it is revealed that mothers, more so than fathers, are using websites such as Facebook to stay connected with emigrated family members.

For example, the gender imbalance is illustrated when Rosin and Dermot's[1] accounts are compared. Rosin's brother Brian moved from Ireland to Australia two years ago and social networking opens up new possibilities for social capital which are unrelated to the geographical place each lives or the geographical distance that separates them. In this regard, Rosin explains that by seeing her brother's photos and online status updates, she feels that he is still living close by her despite the fact he is now living in Australia.

Rosin says:

> "I don't have to be online chatting with him all the time but with Facebook and seeing his photos and posts it feels like he is just over the road from me, well apart from the sand and sun" (Research notes).

This is a very different account to that of Dermot:

> "I have no interest but my wife does. She keeps in contact with our son in Australia and also my sister in Australia and brother in Canada" (Research notes).

This female investment in global family social capital is not something that is unique to the social networking era. Traditionally mothers, as opposed to fathers,

---

1. These quotations come from the research I conducted from 2010 through 2011 in rural Ireland.

have been the main driving force when it comes to connections with wider kin (Dill, 1998; Moore, 1990). Thus while global family social capital might be unique to contemporary society it is governed by traditional gender roles and practices.

Indeed the study reveals that younger females in the household are often the people who equip mothers with the skills to navigate through the world of social networking. For example, Rosin was unsure of how to use Facebook and this condition was reversed by her daughter Emma:

> "The only reason I started using it was to keep in touch with my brother Brian and kids who are in Australia. Emma, [my daughter] was saying to me go onto it. Then one day Emma set me up on it. She's great and keeps me right on the computer" (Research notes).

Here Emma helps familiarize her mother with the world of social networking. Therefore, while teenagers often provide the rest of the family with technical-computing help, more so than any other age group (Kiesler, Zdaniuk, Lundmark, & Kraut, 2000), this study shows that in terms of social networking, this help is often given by female teenagers.

In other accounts it is the individual who is emigrating that encourages the use of social networking. However, it is striking that the invitation is extended to the females in the family circle. Before emigrating, Carla's niece invites her to be her friend online:

> "...she was so sad leaving that before she left she got us to agree, us her aunts and her mum, that Facebook would be our contact place. She had a Beebo account but for some reason preferred that we stay in touch with her on Facebook. I found from my own experience it was full of drivel and I stayed on it for her even though it wasn't my cup of tea" (Research notes).

Carla shows that Facebook provides a 'contact point' where family members can stay in touch with those who have emigrated. Aunts have traditionally played a vital role in young people's lives (in an offline sense) in various ways, as "a teacher, role model, confidante, savvy peer, and second mother" (Ellingson & Sotirin, 2006, p. 483). Therefore, even if the bulk addition of aunts on line by nieces is motivated, as in Carla's niece's case, by a reluctance to leave home; it is possible that after the initial emigration period the online friendships will remain active.

3. Rural fathers' lack of interest in social networking

Throughout the study, fathers display less interest in immersing themselves in the world of social networking. Bobby explains that:

> "I work a bit with computers and although I am an amateur I know a fair bit about them but I'm not into Facebook or have any inclination to be" (Research notes).

While Bobby understands the mechanics of computing he, like Dermot, has no motivation to use Facebook. As 97% of UK households with children now have internet access (Dutton, Blank, & Groselj, 2013), it appears the lack of uptake by fathers is not as a result of poor availability but possibly a lack of desire. This situation calls for more study.

This lack of interest in social networking on the part of fathers seems to relate to the perception that social networking is a time-wasting activity that displaces physical work. Brenda describes her husband's zero tolerance approach to her son spending hours at a time on Facebook:

> "But the thing is when my husband comes home he'll go for him [her son] because he doesn't get this sitting around thing. He would rather see him spending his spare time doing the lawn or something rather than being on Facebook" (Research notes).

Similarly, Colette says of her father:

> "When I'm in the house I do go on it all the time. God yeah it's something I do like just breathing. Like she (her mum Sheila) finds that weird cus Mum you're not on it with friends that much. Dad knows nothing about Facebook or how many friends I have, how much I'm on it but he still gives me all this 'back in the day business.' He goes on about how young people weren't like sitting around gossiping on computers they hadn't time they were always made to work" (Research notes).

Colette's father frequently takes issue with the time she spends online. He has no desire to become more knowledgeable about her online life but he is convinced that it is causing a time displacement in terms of physical work.

While fathers in this study demonstrate little interest in Facebook, in other instances a new found interest is ignited by a major change to family life. For example, in the post divorce family, fathers often, due to physical separation, employ Facebook to maintain contact with their children. Facebook is an extremely social tool for fathers and children to communicate, especially when the mother-father relationship is poor or nonexistent.

For example, Brian has been using Facebook since his divorce two years ago. His online communication with his two children compensates for spending less time with them. The appeal of social networking is twofold. First, in Brian's case, he communicates with his children through private chat and shares photos with them. Second, it avoids the social awkwardness of having to speak to their mother or her boyfriend. He states: "Facebook is a way I get to keep in touch with my kids without having to make small talk with my ex-wife and her boyfriend on the landline" (Research notes).

Observations in the pre-social networking era notes the move from full-time to part-time fatherhood is often difficult to come to terms with (Kruk, 1994). In Brian's case it is shown that the continuous communication on Facebook (viewing comments on others pages, status updates, etc.) smoothes this transition. In terms of global social capital, it also opens up new networks which were previously unavailable. Indeed, Brian notes this when he says he probably would have not gone on Facebook if his family circumstances had stayed the same: "I now have access to a whole new network where I now can keep in touch with family and friends living abroad" (Research notes).

4.   Limitations

This study has two notable limitations. First, all of the participating fathers were over 45 years old. It might be the case that a very different picture would emerge in the case of younger fathers and their use of social networking. This is likely given the fact that social networking is "highest among 16-24 year olds [...but] decreases with age" (OFCOM, 2008, p. 5) and in the UK almost half of those over the age of fifty five have never been online (BBC, 2011).

Second, today's technology changes rapidly. The young people and their families participating in this study were interviewed during 2010 and 2011. At that time participants had only limited access to broadband. However, more recent research shows rural broadband in Northern Ireland exceeds even that of urban uptake (OFCOM, 2013). Therefore rural fathers may be a more defined group of Internet users given the time that has passed.

5.   Advancing social capital theory

Despite these limitations the evidence presented in this chapter advances social capital theory in two ways. First, it identifies and explains a new level of social capital, namely global family social capital. The existence of global social capital makes questionable the assumptions that dominate the traditional social capital literature. For example, early social capital theory had a strong focus on joint mother-father investment for social capital production. In contrast, this chapter suggests thatglobal family social capital exists with little to no male input and should flourish just as well in the variety of modern family forms beyond the nuclear family. Unlike early claims about social capital, non-intact families or lone motherhood does not pose a threat to social capital. This is because mothers and daughters are the catalyst behind global family social capital and males have little input in creating and sustaining it.

Second, the use of technology means that social capital is no longer rooted in place and location as was the case during the pre-social networking era. For example, despite their very different applications and interpretations of social capital, Coleman (1988) and Putnam (2000) both argue its quality is something that varies between countries and nations. For Coleman (1988), social capital was, as illustrated in his classic example of the distinction between New York and Jerusalem, very different from one country and cultural tradition to the next. Additionally, while Putnam's (2000) central concern was dwindling social capital in the United States, he does draw distinctions between the quality of social capital between North and South Italy. Given that in the social networking era, people, such as Carla's niece or Rosin's brother, can connect with family members regardless of being separated by geographical distance, social capital now transcends space and place, and connections are not as limited by geography as they were in the past.

6.   Conclusion: being offline increases rural disadvantage

In one sense by remaining offline some rural fathers are circumventing the dangers linked to social networking such as lack of privacy and risk taking (Stephenson-Abetz & Holman, 2012). However, they also miss out on a number of opportunities to use the Internet to suit their needs, make life easier, more enjoyable and productive. The UK government has welcomed technological advances such as broadband for its "ability to transform our lives –whether in business, education or in how we use our leisure time" and for being an essential resource to compete in the global knowledge economy (Tony Blair, 2005). Generally, the broad aim is to make the UK the most digitally capable nation in the world (Dutton et al., 2013). While the world races further and faster online, it appears that individuals lagging behind will be disadvantaged economically, educationally and socially.

The negative social impact of not being online may be heightened by one's location, such as living in a rural area. Traditionally the rural was perhaps perceived as "backward", "disconnected" and "isolated" from the perspective of the people that live there (Research notes). Internet use overcomes the disadvantage of being physically remote from family and improves the lives of rural residents (Valentine & Holloway, 2001). The Internet and social networking has the potential to 'connect' rural dwellers to a larger world. In this study rural fathers are missing out on a range of opportunities for increased sociability in this larger online world. From a social capital perspective a failure to connect with globally dispersed family means one misses out on additional emotional support (bonding social capital) and informational support (bridging social capital). By tapping into this extra reserve of social capital and particularly bonding social capital for increased emotional support, Northern Ireland males might increase their health and well being. Presently, males in Northern Ireland are at a distinct gender disadvantage in terms of health and well-being, and are five times more likely to die by suicide (Richardson, Clarke, & Fowler, 2013).

Additionally, from an economic perspective the failure to nurture online connections may give males a disadvantage in the global economy and the modern workplace where skills, such as networking and sustaining online relations are valued therein. This poses a major problem considering technology has a fast pace of change. It appears that the longer one remains offline, the more difficult it may be to catch up with technological advancements.

The examples presented in this chapter support other rural research across Europe. It has been widely noted that age determines the way in which the benefits of social networking are distributed among rural populations. For example, it is young people who most frequently use social networking in rural Wales (Milbourne & Kitchen, 2014). Similarly, in rural Finland, Internet use (in general) is a routine and everyday practice for young people but is not widely used by older age groups (Kilpeläinen & Seppänen, 2014). None of these studies, however, have noted a greater use of social networking among rural mothers than fathers. It would be interesting to establish if similar gender patterns are observed in other rural regions of other countries or if these gender patterns are something unique to Northern Ireland.

References

Albergotti, R. (2014, July 4). Facebook study poor: Sandberg. *The Australian*.

BBC. (2011, October 24). Give an hour: Opening up a new world. *BBC*. Retrieved from http:// www.bbc.co.uk/news/uk-england-london-15370614

Blair, T. (2005, April 4). Britain hits broadband milestone. *BBC News*. Retrieved from http:// news.bbc.co.uk/1/hi/technology/4408219.stm

Boyd, D. M., & Ellison, N. B. (2007). Social network sites: Definition, history and scholarship. *Journal of Computer-Mediated Communication, 13*(1), 210-230. doi:10.1111/j.1083-6101.2007.00393.x

Coleman, J. S. (1988). Social capital in the creation of human capital. *The American Journal of Sociology, 94*(Supplement), 95-120. doi:10.1086/228943

Dill, B. T. (1998). Fictive kin, paper sons, and compadrazgo: Women of color and the struggle for family survival. *Journal of Family History, 13*(4), 415-431.

Dutton, W. H., Blank, G., & Groselj, D. (2013). *Cultures of the Internet: The Internet in Britain. Oxford Internet Survey 2013*. Oxford: University of Oxford.

Ellingson, L. L., & Sotirin, P. J. (2006). Exploring young adults' perspectives on communication with aunts. *Journal of Social and Personal Relationships, 23*(3), 483-501. doi:10.1177/0265407506064217

Halpern, D. (2005). *Social Capital*. Cambridge: Polity Press.

Kiesler, S., Zdaniuk, B., Lundmark, V., & Kraut, R. (2000). Troubles with the Internet. The dynamics of help at home. *Human Computer Interaction, 15*(4), 323-351. doi:10.1207/S15327051HCI1504_2

Kilpeläinen, A., & Seppänen, M. (2014). Information technology and everyday life in aging rural villages. *Journal of Rural Studies, 33*, 1-8. doi:10.1016/j.jrurstud.2013.10.005

Kruk, E. (1994). The disengaged noncustodial father: Implications for social work practice with the divorced family. *Social Work, 39*(1), 15-25.

Milbourne, P., & Kitchen, L. (2014). Rural Mobilities: connecting movements and fixity in rural places. *Journal of Rural Studies, 34*, 326-336. doi:10.1016/j.jrurstud.2014.01.004

Moore, G. (1990). Structural determinants of men's and women's personal networks. *American Sociological Review, 55*, 726-735. doi:10.2307/2095868

OFCOM. (2008). Social networking: *A quantitative and qualitative research report into attitudes, behaviours and use*. Office of Communications. Retrieved from http://news.bbc.co.uk/2/shared/bsp/hi/pdfs/02_04_08_ofcom.pdf

OFCOM. (2013). *The communications market report: Northern Ireland*. Office of Communications. Retrieved from http://stakeholders.ofcom.org.uk/market-data-research/market-data/communications-market-reports/cmr13/northern-ireland/

Putnam, R. D. (2000). *Bowling alone: The collapse and revival of American community*. New York: Simon & Schuster.

Rice, A. (2014). *An investigation into emerging social relations among rural young people: The relationship between social networking and individual, family and community social capital*. Unpublished PhD thesis. Belfast: Queens University Belfast.

Richardson, N., Clarke, N., & Fowler, C. (2013). *A report on the ALL-Ireland young men and suicide project. Men's health forum in Ireland*. CommunityNI. Retrieved from http://www.communityni.org/news/all-ireland-young-men-and-suicide-project-report-launched

Stephenson-Abetz, J., & Holman, A. 2012. Home is where the heart is: Facebook and the negotiation of old and new during the transition to college. *Western Journal of Communication, 76*(2), 175-193. doi:10.1080/10570314.2011.654309

Valentine, G., & Holloway, S. L. (2001). A window on the wider world? Rural children's use of information and communication technologies. *Journal of Rural Studies, 17*(4), 383-394. doi:10.1016/S0743-0167(01)00022-5

3 Online religious advertising: The case of Australian Christian youth festivals

Paul Emerson Teusner[1]

Abstract

This chapter explores the changing nature of Christian denominational discourse in an Australian context as informed by Internet technologies. It will take as its case study three Internet sites developed and published for the promotion of three separate Christian youth festivals held in Australia between July 2008 and January 2009, undertaking a discursive analysis of their structures, content and design to examine how Internet and institutional religion interact in delivering a Christian message to contemporary Australian young people. The analysis will show that, despite the diverse theological positions, convention goals and approaches to the Internet, all three sites are surprisingly similar in form, while the content stays true to denominational tradition. The study raises questions about the intersection of technology, culture and religion and in particular, how the contours of Christian diversity in Australia are being redrawn, so that membership to a particular denomination, institution or group can no longer define what kind of Christian any Australian is.

Keywords: online religion, Australian Christian festivals, youth and Internet.

1. E-mail address: paulteusner@me.com

How to cite this chapter: Emerson Teusner, P. (2014). Online religious advertising: The case of Australian Christian youth festivals. In J. D. James (Ed.), *The Internet and the Google age: Prospects and perils* (pp. 63-80). Dublin: Research-publishing. net. doi:10.14705/rpnet.2014.000178

1. Introduction

While computer-mediated communication technologies have been in use by some businesses, academic and government organisations in Australia since the 1980s, the Internet as we know it now was not available to the household until the acquisition of business-usage rights by the then largest Australian telecommunications company, Telstra, in 1995. From then until the late 1990s, commercial ISPs numbering around 600 independent businesses were offering the Internet into Australian homes, to the extent that by the end of 1998, 1.3 million households were online (Clarke, 2004).

By 2004, 95 percent of Australian homes with parents and young people considered the Internet a normal household expense, according to the *Sydney Morning Herald*, a major Australian daily paper (mentioned in Barker, 2004), and the Australian Bureau of Statistics recorded that 84 percent of all Australians aged 18-24 used the Internet (ABS, 2004). It is little surprise then that the Internet forms an important part of the advertising and promotion strategy of Australian organisations. While not necessarily the most effective medium for advertising, in comparison to television, radio, newspapers and magazines, the Internet has become an important complement to these media for a number of reasons. Any interest in a product or service aroused by a television, radio or print advertisement can be maintained by directing the audience to a web site for further information. An Internet domain is a permanent advertising space, usually cheaper to maintain than other advertising sources, for a business that sells more than one product or service and can help build brand loyalty. On the other side of the coin, interactive functions, such as online surveys and polls, registration facilities, and online competitions (plus other more invasive and nefarious data-mining strategies) enable organisations to gain information about their market that will better inform their range of products and services and other advertising strategies.

Church organisations find in the Internet an effective medium for the promotion of events, such as youth festivals, reaching out to an audience beyond their congregations, and maintaining interest through interactivity and news feeding.

2. An Australian Christian story

The Christian churches have sat in an uneasy place in Australian society ever since Europeans arrived to the continent in the eighteenth century. It took many years and much pressure from immigrants for British churches to consider the communities of convicts, emancipists and free settlers as mission fields (Breward, 1988, p. 1). Rather than conscientious opposition that grew in North American societies, it was apathy that halted the establishment of a national Church in the colonies.

The same apathy allowed for the growth of religious diversity and the development of a unique religious character for the land that would be a nation. Colonial governments supported the importation of both Protestant and Roman Catholic clergy and professionals to build charities for migrants and freed convicts, the majority of whom were Irish Catholics (Breward, 1988, pp. 11, 13).

The copper and gold boom of the mid 1800's attracted both miners and evangelists who gained followers more by their practical piety than formal theological education. It was in this period that Methodist and Baptist churches grew rapidly by the deployment of lay preachers (Breward, 1988, p. 28). Finke and Stark (2005) notice a similar expansion in the history of the United States' expansion. In the absence of an established national church, as in Europe, religious diversity thrived and the growth of denominational communities were fuelled by a process akin to market forces: those that grew were those that could provide religious products that the wider community would be attracted to consume (Finke & Stark, 2005, pp. 15-20).

Even this early in the history of White Australia, common sense pointed to an ecumenical Christian presence, if at least a common Protestantism. Anglicans, Presbyterians and Wesleyans shared resources to build churches in marginal areas, including the support of clergy (Breward, 1988, pp. 23-24). This common sense survived into the next century, where a federated Australia saw the union of all Lutheran churches (previously divided by ethnic origins), a Baptist

Union, and an Australian Anglican General Synod (Breward, 1988, p. 66). Even Methodism, Congregationalism, and most Presbyterian communities were lost to a Uniting Church in Australia.

It is argued that this ecumenical sensibility fuelled the separation of church from state in the nation's development. For example, a passion for justice united Christians to the campaign of state-funded education in the second half of the nineteenth century that led to the dissolution of most Protestant schools. It could have ended all sectarianism, but it paved the way for a Roman Catholic system that aimed for a religious alternative to secularist education, and then new Protestant schools that aimed for prestige and refinement (Breward, 1988, pp. 32-33). The same passion in Christian community service led to the ideal that the professional skill is more important than the religious affiliation of service agencies' staff, and would eventually mean the independence of many from their Christian roots (Breward, 1988, pp. 86-87). Examples include the Brotherhood of St Lawrence, Mission Australia and the Australian Workers Union. Even organisations that carry a denominational label, such as Anglicare and UnitingCare, ensure the culture of the workplace remains primarily secular, even where chaplains are employed.

Against the historical backdrop of consensual secularism and latent ecumenism, the mid 1900's saw a convergence of various global social and political factors that led to a watershed in Australian religious history, among the effects of which the Australian emerging church now sees itself. These include, but are not exhausted by, the Billy Graham crusades, the Second Vatican Council, the arrival of television, the Asian Wars, the World Council of Churches, the Death of God, and communism.

Evangelical crusades and revivals have been with Australians since before the Gold Rush. They focused on simple pragmatic doctrines balanced by fervour for community harmony and service. Evangelists were often gifted with more charisma than formal education, and understood the plight of their congregations. Billy Graham entered Australia with the same properties, but his style led to a new flavour of Evangelicalism that will be the key characteristic for Evangelicalism in that century and the next. Graham's works had earned him many devotees in North America, and arrived down under with a large capital outlay to produce large musical and dramatic events in our capital cities that drew unusually large crowds (Breward, 1988, p. 77). With Graham came the idea that the spectacle is as important as the message.

Graham's crusade, like other evangelistic pursuits to follow, was worded in the language of new media of the period: television. Clark (2003, p. 30) notes the four main tenets of Evangelicalism are that

- humans are in need of salvation;
- Christians are charged with bringing others to the faith;
- the Bible is free of errors and must be understood literally; and
- the Rapture will mark the end of days, vindicating the plight of believers.

As television became the dominant form of mass media in Western culture, the late twentieth century saw both religious and secular polities increasingly submissive to its discursive structure. Television was, as it still is, a medium packed with stories of good versus evil, where even journalism shows contain a narrative and ritual structure that is filled with drama. The Evangelical Gospel found a comfortable place among the messages beamed into homes of this period.

Australian broadcasting regulations of the 1960's onwards allowed a space for religious programming, even if it were just among the screening of commercials. Mainstream Protestant and Catholic churches lacked a voice of authority for the new media environment, and struggled with how to approach it ethically and structurally. The Christian Television Association was developed to deal with these issues on the behalf of the major denominations and became a well-known Christian presence in Australian television until regulations were relaxed in the 1990's, making Christian broadcasts more expensive, having to compete for air-time in the same way as other community and commercial organisations. Now the newly named Christian Television Australia focuses its resources on a digital channel, with rarely run special programmes on free-to-air.

It seems now that the once-small evangelical Christian voice is the great winner in Australian broadcasting deregulation. Its energies are not wasted by the strict authority regimes and ethical debates that confronted the mainstream churches (Lehikoinen, 2003, pp. 165-166). American televangelism, such as the ministries of Oral Roberts, Pat Robertson, Marilyn Hickey and Benny Hinn, had enough resources to buy air time on Australian television. Their common message was that the Bible is given directly by God and so must be read with a literal eye, that prayer brings rewards to the true believer who is persecuted by a secular world unprotected from Satan's influence and is called to bring moral regeneration until the end of days, which are imminent. Though a very marginal Christian worldview, the rituals contained within the television programming, together with the ritual acts adopted by its consumers, helped legitimate the religious identity of viewers as part of a global movement (Alexander, 1994, pp. 3-5).

Evangelical Christianity has, since Billy Graham, been seen as a rapidly growing movement with a strong successful voice in Australian society, to the shame of Catholicism and mainstream Protestantism. Television has helped, not just by carrying the message, but by reinforcing the shape of the Australian religious milieu as a market, where religious identity is built by consumption, and where the success of an organisation is dependent, albeit somewhat, on the marketability of its products. This is indeed the basis of criticism of Australia's mega churches, such as Hillsong in Sydney and Adelaide's Paradise Church, labelled by some in the emerging church movement as more akin to businesses than religious communities.

Television is not the only transforming force of changes in Australia's Christian landscape in the mid and late twentieth century. While ecumenical activities engaged dialogue between established denominations with increasing fervour, political debates asked Christians to take sides, producing divides within denominational structures. Whatever differences divided Christians into Catholics and Protestants would become less important than those that defined a "left-wing" and a "right-wing", or a Liberal versus a Conservative Christian.

The Second Vatican Council spanned three years and involved two Popes, ending in 1965. It changed the face of the Roman Catholic Church, opening its doors to alternative methods of theological inquiry, greater freedoms of expression for congregational brothers and sisters, and interest in inter-denominational and inter-faith dialogue. In response to its global power, Catholics in Australia found a seat in the Australian Council of Churches (now known as the National Council of Church in Australia) and involvement in joint theological training organisations, such as the United Faculty of Theology and the Melbourne College of Divinity. Economic prosperity, social mobility, free education and urban sprawl since the 1950's closed distances between Catholics and Protestants in both geography and class. Pure Catholic families were growing at a slower rate, inter-denominational marriages were becoming normal (Breward, 1993, p. 67).

But one Papal Encyclical would cause a disagreement among Catholics, creating a divide that is not yet resolved. *Humanae Vitae*, subtitled "On The Regulation Of Birth" was written by Pope Paul VI and released in 1968, reaffirming traditional teaching and unequivocally condemning contraception and abortion. Many Catholics began to question the infallibility of the Papacy, and clergy met those confessing to the sin of using contraception with acknowledgment that it was a matter of personal conscience (Breward, 1988, p. 73).

In Australia as in other parts of the world, political movements evoked responses by Christians that separated them from others. They would include the anti-war movement and feminism of the 1960's and 1970's, and the environmentalism and the gay and lesbian rights movement of the 1980's and 1990's. Wuthnow (1989) describes the distinction between pro and con among believers as arising out of a perceived gap between political values and behaviour (pp. 32-34). The Liberals attacked the behaviour of government while the Conservatives critiqued values. Conservatives wanted out of political involvement, focusing more on changing personal beliefs, while Liberals saw this was not enough for the Church's witness to the world.

Generations in this half of the century had grown more educated than those before, and had allowed themselves to question the authority of their denominational patriarchs. Not surprising then that 1963 saw the peak of participation in traditional religious communities in Australia. The Death of God movement of the 1960's, informed by the works of Barth and Bonhoeffer, led in part by the 1963 publication of *Honest to God*, written by John Robinson, then Anglican Bishop of Woolwich, criticised contemporary Christian theology and claimed that while traditional images of God were absent in the secular world, a sense of the sacred can no longer be found among the cloisters of the Church (Altizer & Hamilton, 1966, pp. 28-36, 39). Instead, the Christian way of life should be found by leaving the church and going into secular life. Radical liberal groups, including the Australian Student Christian Movement, claimed the failure of Australia's mainline churches to listen to and speak to the world (Breward, 1993, p. 169).

While Liberal Christians laid their attacks on the Church for distancing itself from society, in later decades radical Conservatives set their aim for governments. Organisations such as Catch the Fire Ministries and the Australian Prayer Networks did well to catch the attention of state and federal politicians in their claims for a presence of Christian spirit and fervour in the running of the country. Some Christians organised themselves into political parties, calling for Australia's moral and spiritual renewal, and a return to "family values". Such parties include Family First and the Christian Democratic Party. Due partly to the strong presence of Evangelical churches in mainstream media, prominent politicians have found in them a support for a conservative agenda, and not least the country's then Prime Minister, the Hon. John Howard, and former Treasurer, the Hon. Peter Costello. Mainstream news media has responded to politicians' interest in these groups to turn their own attention to religious debates happening in denominations and the impact on Australian life. The place of religion in political life, especially in the face of a growing Muslim immigrant and refugee population, and terrorism post-9/11, is a popular article for consideration by any radio or television news program.

It is growing apparent that Australians define the Christian identity less by their involvement in a denomination and more by their stance on a variety of political, religious and social issues, like abortion, sexual morality, the ordination of women and homosexuals, stem-cell research and our responsibility to the environment. People draw from a large market of sources for resources to form religious identity outside their local religious community and its parent denominational authority. These views are still dividing people within traditional institutional structures and encouraging alliances among previously separated groups.

The Roman Catholic Church sits as the largest Christian denomination in Australia, accounting for half of church attendants in 2001, according to the National Church Life Survey. They are followed by the Anglicans and the Uniting Church. Yet these denominations also represent the shrinking mainstream church in Australia. The Catholics saw a 13 percent decrease in participation between 1996 and 2001, while Uniting Church numbers dropped by 11 percent. The Anglican Church lost two percent of its overall population in this period, though it is believed that while the Sydney Archdiocese saw "significant" growth, the rest of Australia suffered more than 10 percent loss of membership. It is too soon to say that Christianity is dying in this country however. The same survey sees rapid growth in Pentecostal churches, by 20 percent for the Apostolic churches and Assemblies of God, and by 42 percent in the Christian City Churches (Bellamy & Castle, 2004, pp. 5-8).

It seems, however, that not even Pentecostal churches can retain young people (i.e. those aged 15-24). The National Church Life Survey records that Pentecostal churches could only retain 5.5 percent of its young people between 1991 and 2001, while 15 percent of all its members moved from this family of denominations to other Christian communities. Mainstream Protestant churches were equally unable to keep its young, retaining only 4 percent in the five years to 2001 (Sterland, Powell, & Castle, 2006, pp. 10-12).

3. The question

While more than half of young Australians say they believe in God, there is generally a low interest in religious participation, and they hold strong beliefs in the freedom of religious expression and moral relativism (Mason, Singleton,

& Webber, 2007). Given that young people spend at least forty hours weekly engaged in mass media (Brooks, 2007, p. 23), denominational authorities have much to compete with in teaching their young how to grow into a Christian life.

The question I would like to present for exploration is, then, twofold. To what extent are traditional denominational discourses surviving in a contemporary Internet environment? Is there a textual and symbolic exchange between Christian discourses and other discourses operating online that attract and engage young people's interaction?

Approaching these questions, I will use as case studies the Internet sites associated with three Australian Christian youth festivals: the National Christian Youth Convention (http://ncyc.org.au/), organised by the Uniting Church, to be held in January 2009, the World Day of Youth (http://www.wyd2008.org/), organised by the Catholic Church and held in July 2008, and the Hillsong United Youth Conference (http://www2.hillsong.com/hillsongunitedyouthconference/), also held in July 2008 and organised by Hillsong, a congregation of the Assemblies of God (aka Australian Christian Churches).

4.   The method

A discursive method of analysis is employed to approach the question. This method is informed by the work of Gee (2005), who defines discourse as "ways of combining and integrating language, actions, interactions, ways of thinking, believing, valuing, and using various symbols, tools, and objects to enact a particular sort of socially recognizable identity" (p. 21). Moreover, I am informed by the model of multimodal analysis developed by Kress and van Leeuwen (2001), who assert that discourses are present not just in text, but in design, production and distribution (pp. 4-8, 42-43). According to their model, it is important to acknowledge that discourses lie in:

- the lines of authority and communication between site creators and the people, communities and institutions on whose behalf they speak;

- the placement of word, image, sound and other forms of text on each web page, and the structure of pages within each site;

- the technology itself, and perceptions of its usage and values imposed on it by both producers and consumers.

For the sake of conciseness, this study is primarily concerned with text and its placement in the design of the web pages being considered. Four types of religious discourse are studied:

- discourses of *proclamation*: statements and other text intended to connect the reader to religious belief or doctrine;

- discourses of *identity*: statements and other text intended to connect the reader to a group identity, such as a denomination or movement;

- discourses of *participation*: statements and other text intended to connect the reader to other readers, or event organisers;

- discourses of *activation*: statements and other text intended to connect the reader to a sense of Christian purpose or religious life.

5.   The survey

All three sites, from here on referred to as the NCYC site, the Hillsong site and the WYD site, for brevity, use Content Management System (CMS) programming to effect a site design. CMS makes site creation easier for producers, who can make simple changes to text without having to reload the site's entire data, provide uniformity across all pages within a site, and offer site readers/users simple navigation tools (Seadle, 2006). The use of CMS also makes each site's display fairly similar to each other. All sites have a picture or animated header (banner), and either a topbar or sidebar containing navigation links to each page within the site.

The banners of the Hillsong and WYD sites contain streams of images. On the Hillsong banner pictures of young people having fun and listening to music or dancing in a concert audience are juxtaposed with images of poverty and loneliness in foreign deserts or urban landscapes. The words of Mark 16:15, "Go into all the world and preach the good news to all creation", appear in the centre of these images, with "into all the world" specifically highlighted. On the WYD site banner, the words of Acts 1:8, "You will receive power when the Holy Spirit has come upon you and you will be my witnesses", sit above images of Sydney's skyline juxtaposed with images of young people conversing, laughing, dancing and carrying flags of various nations.

The only image in the NCYC site's banner is a Uniting Church logo. Words scattered over the banner (such as "greatness", "seeds", "interpretation" and "disciples") are, however, composed as graffiti on a wall, or scribbles on a chalkboard. The idea is, I believe, to construct a sense of under-culture, or subculture, as if the words are "dirty". Pictorial images are sparse in the body of the NCYC site's content. Text relating to all four discourses is apparent throughout the site's pages. Consider these discourses of proclamation:

> "NCYC09 is the time and place where delegates converge as the beloved of God from all places to hear the Good News of hope, peace and justice".

> "Overall the key ideas that shape the theology within the Biblical texts for NCYC09 are about identity and radical discipleship. Radical discipleship is a perspective or approach to Christian spirituality that sees Jesus as the "root" for Christian life and utilises him as the key to biblical interpretation. Participation in the Good News and salvation brings both personal and social change" (NCYC).

Of participation:

> "Delegates come together for a week to discover, celebrate and deepen the faith and unity we have in Jesus Christ. We converge to live as an intentional Christian community for a week, we have the opportunity to

converge with the Good News in our everyday lives and with our home faith communities, and ultimately we will each converge with God" (NCYC).

And of activation:

"NCYC is more than just a week away in January. Delegates return to homes, congregations and schools hyped, inspired and challenged from what they've experienced –motivated to carry out God's will in the church and wider community" (NCYC).

Discourses of activation appear to be lacking in printed word form in the WYD site. Proclamation discourse exists in some places, for example:

"The logo distils the essence of the theme for WYD08 and highlights the promise made by Jesus to set fire upon the Earth by the power of the Holy Spirit which inspires the pilgrims who come to Australia, to believe and witness to Him" (WYD).

However, discourses of identity are ubiquitous in this site. Readers are connected to a sense of belonging to a global Catholic Church, by reference to the Pope and his clergy, both in word and in image. It is interesting to see photographs of conference staff dressed in official clerical clothing along images of young people in casual dress. Identity discourse in the Hillsong site is more sparse, and centred on the history of the Hillsong Conference project:

"As a passionate force of young people, we embarked on the journey of JAM United a decade ago. Such humble beginnings these were [...]. Yet over the years, the uncontainable faith continued to grow and together we have crossed uncharted territory as thousands of lives have been changed. Today we stand, toes wriggling with excitement at the edge of a new chapter. Cos [sic], just like God renamed his people to fit a new season, JAM United has just gone to a whole new level, now to be known as the Hillsong United Conference!" (Hillsong).

Rather than a connection to a global community, the Hillsong site attracts readers to a sense of belonging to a local organisational story. Likewise, the NCYC site contains identity discourse that is more historical than geographic, yet extends the tradition beyond the bounds of the organisation itself, to a wider Christian history:

> "Radical discipleship has similarities with liberation theology and the Anabaptist tradition, all expecting personal and social transformation as the Kingdom of God is realised in the here and now. Popular figures associated with the movement include Ched Myers, John Smith, Athol Gill, Dorothy Day, Martin Luther King Jr, Dietrich Bonhoeffer, Dave Andrews, John Hirt, Merrill Kitchen, Robert McAfee Brown, Jeanette Mathews, Thorwald Lorenzen, Tim Costello, Ross Langmead, Ashley Barker, and our own John Uren" (NCYC).

As mentioned before, the NCYC site has little images beyond the Uniting Church logo; images and sounds exist in YouTube(TM) videos, mp3-file podcasts and blogs that are embedded in the site. These embedded objects tell stories of the event's preparation, personal stories told by organisers, and invitations for comments and submissions of users' own content. Such embedded objects are also found in the Hillsong site, and are mainly sermons by guest speakers and music clips of the event's bands, intended to inspire audiences through activation discourses to respond in their daily life outside the event.

The NCYC site has official pages on social networking sites like Facebook(TM) and Flickr(TM), and encourages users to visit these pages and contribute. The WYD site also promotes a social networking site, called xt3, created specifically for participants of the WYD event.

6.   Findings

Considering a survey of the structure, banner titles, printed words and visual texts, embedded objects and links to external Internet sites, certain findings may be proposed.

In all sites, religious text is framed by texts present in popular culture. Images of young people playing music, dancing in concert audiences, walking on the beach, laughing and having fun are set against church logos, biblical verses and photographs of clergy. The body of the text is casual, fraught with slang, and set against backdrops such as television screens and graffiti walls.

Yet each site emphasises a particular type of religious discourse. The NCYC site favours participation discourse, calling users to connect with other participants, and even its organisers, to create a community of people with a common story.

For the WYD site, the emphasis is on identity discourse, calling people from around the world to be unified under a common symbol. Activation discourse is favoured in the Hillsong site, calling users to join in a common message and take it out to their own worlds.

These discourses are more evident in audiovisual text embedded in the sites' pages, and to a lesser extent, in the links to external sites than in the printed word. They are present in the juxtaposition with images of popular culture, framed by an overall image of youthfulness, giving value to the world and way of life of young people.

7. Conclusion: the intersection of Australian Christianity, youth culture and the Internet

In 2005, Australian church organisations pooled finances together and employed an advertising agency to create a series of radio and television commercials, plus a website that offered information about the communities and its people. The advertising campaign was titled "Jesus –all about life" and featured young adults, parents and older people expressing their interest in the person of Jesus Christ. Every television and radio advertisement intentionally omitted any reference to the churches involved, and even Christianity itself.

For the first time in Australian media, Christians refused to portray themselves in their religious promotion. Only in the website was there a small reference to Australian Christian churches, and only links to their own denominational website and contact information.

The ad campaign showed a realisation that Australians were, by-and-large, indifferent to Christian identity and community, though they had some interest in faith and spirituality.

The WYD site has pictures of the Pope and his clergy, and the NCYC site has a Uniting Church logo on each page, yet denominational demarcations are by no other means made explicit in these sites[1]. None of these sites promote, or even offer for consideration, belonging to a particular denomination.

Yet the traditions of each denomination are found in the type of religious discourse emphasised in each site. The formation of a Christian message for the medium is founded to some extent on a denominational history, though only the characteristics of that history and integrity are open to the site's readers and users.

Just like the "Jesus –all about life" ad campaign, these sites represent an endeavour to capture the audience of Internet communities with certain characteristics, people who are interested in faith with a certain bent, purpose or claim, rather than a denominational label.

These sites, like the events they promote, recognise the Australian religious community is not defined by denominational or institutional membership or participation. They show us, however, that the Australian Christian landscape is still rich in diversity, and seeking new ways to talk about themselves.

---

1. It can be argued that the youth conference web pages are not the sites to look for denominational identities, as denominational identities are enforced and reinforced in the practice of rites of passage and worship orders of the churches. Hence, what is happening in these web pages could be an attempt to draw the youth towards faith so as to make them members of the concerned church community in order to give allegiance to the denomination. Therefore, youth conferences could be seen more like initiation ceremonies for catching 'fishes of men'.

The Hillsong "Young and Free, Y & F" website through the careful use of slogans and 'branding' is aimed at speaking to the needs and aspirations of modern Australian young people:

> "we are a youth ministry by name, but by identity we are a people who have found hope and salvation [...]. More than a label, Young and Free is also our message and mission. This is a generation called to stand strong in their youth and in their freedom, refusing to allow others to dismiss them for their age, and not allowing the chains of their history to leave them shackled" (http://hillsong.com/youngandfree).

In the same website, the Hillsong Encounter Recounted Conference 2014[1] is promoted with five compelling reasons as to why young people should attend. Again we see that youthful freedom is capitalized and denominational associations, deliberately avoided.

References

ABS. (2004). *Year Book of Australia, 2004.* Canberra: Australian Bureau of Statistics.

Alexander, B. C. (1994). *Televangelism reconsidered: Ritual in the search for human community.* Atlanta: Scholars Press.

Altizer, T. J. J., Hamilton, W. (1966). *Radical Theology and the Death of God.* Indianapolis: Bobbs-Merrill.

Barker, G. (2004). *One in five children stalked on net.* Sydney: Sydney Morning Herald.

Bellamy, J., & Castle, K. (2004). *NCLS Occasional Paper 3: 2001 Church Attendance Estimates.* Sydney: NCLS Research.

Breward, I. (1988). *Australia: The most Godless place under heaven?* Melbourne: Lutheran Publishing House.

Breward, I. (1993). *A History of Australian Churches.* Sydney: Allen & Unwin.

Brooks, K. (2007). Honey, I shrunk the library: Technology, cyberspace and knowledge culture. *Access, 21*(1), 21-26.

---

1. http://hillsong.com/youngandfree/content/yf-blogs/5-reasons-not-to-miss-encounter#.VC7-JdTF9wV

Clark, L. S. (2003). *From angels to aliens: Teenagers, the media, and the supernatural.* New York: Oxford University Press.

Clarke, R. (2004). Origins and nature of the Internet in Australia. *Roger Clarke's Web-Site.* Retrieved from http://www.anu.edu.au/people/Roger.Clarke/II/OzI04.html

Finke, R., & Stark, R. (2005). *The Churching of America, 1776-2005: Winners and losers in our religious economy.* Piscataway Township, NJ: Rutgers University Press.

Gee, J. P. (2005). *An introduction to discourse analysis: Theory and method* (2nd ed.). London: Routledge.

Kress, G., & van Leeuwen, T. (2001). *Multimodal discourse: The modes and media of contemporary communication.* London: Arnold.

Lehikoinen, T. (2003). *Religious media theory: Understanding mediated Faith and Christian applications to modern media.* Jyväskylä: Jyväskylä University Press.

Mason, M., Singleton, A., & Webber, R. (2007). *The spirit of Generation Y: Young people's spirituality in a changing Australia.* Melbourne: John Garratt Publishing.

Seadle, M. (2006). Content management systems. *Library Hi Tech, 24*(1), 5-7.

Sterland, S., Powell, R., & Castle, K. (2006). *NCLS Occasional Paper 8: Inflow and outflow between denominations: 1991 to 2001.* Sydney: NCLS Research.

Wuthnow, R. (1989). *The struggle for America's soul: Evangelicals, liberals, and secularism.* Grand Rapids: Eerdmans.

4 The computer revolution and evangelical mission research and strategy: An historical overview[1]

Michael Jaffarian[2]

Abstract

This chapter consists of a short history of the impact of computer technology on Christian evangelical mission research from the 1970's to the present. The trail winds through World Vision, MARC, the *World Christian Encyclopedia, Operation World*, SIL, OC International, DAWN, Global Mapping International, the AD2000 and Beyond Movement, and Joshua Project. Attention is given to projects in Asia, to some remarkable contributions from and to Silicon Valley, and to the origin of the well known missionary strategic map the '10/40 Window'. It ends with a discussion of tools and tasks, of whether the Internet and computers have helped or harmed the Christian missionary enterprise.

Keywords: missions and technology, computers in the Church, history of Internet in the Church.

1.   Introduction

Mainframes, then minis, then micros, like a blinking, buzzing hoard, computers invaded the countryside of the global human experience, set up occupation, and

---

1. An earlier version of this paper was presented at the Fifth International Lausanne Researchers' Conference, Geelong, Australia in April 2008. Later it was published in the International Bulletin of Missionary Research under the title: "The Computer Revolution and Its Impact on Evangelical Mission Research and Strategy" (in January, 2009, 33,1, pp. 33-37) and is reprinted with amendments with the kind permission of the Editor, Nelson Jennings.

2. E-mail address: emichaeljaffarian@gmail.com

How to cite this chapter: Jaffarian, M. (2014). The Internet and evangelical mission research and strategy: An historical overview. In J. D. James (Ed.), *The Internet and the Google age: Prospects and perils* (pp. 81-98). Dublin: Research-publishing.net. doi: 10.14705/rpnet.2014.000179

instigated change everywhere. They have marched in by the thousands, then by the millions, and then, thanks to the Internet, connected with each other into a vast network like one enormous, pulsing, global brain[1]. The worlds of agriculture, architecture, art, commerce, communication, development, education, engineering, entertainment, finance, government, industry, politics, scholarship, science, sports, warfare, and more will never be the same.

2. Overview of missions, computer usage and mapping

What about the world of Christian mission? Almost all Western missionaries, and many non-Western missionaries, now head to their holy assignments with computers in their baggage, if not clutched in their hands. Much could be said about the impact of computer-aided translation, dubbing, and production of media, email and VoIP communication, Internet-based training, Internet evangelism, non-residential missionaries, on-line missiological academic and historical resources, Web 2.0 social networking, and Web-delivered Christian media –but the focus of this article is on Evangelical global mission research and strategy.

Tools shape tasks, and tasks shape tools. Here is this powerful, influential, even intoxicating tool, the computer. As an astute journalist observed in 1996, "[t]here's no sure way to measure how much the Internet will change our lives, but the most basic truth about technological revolutions is that they change everything they touch" (Ramo, 1996, p. 67).

Consider the saying, "To a man with a hammer, everything looks like a nail"[2]. Maybe when the computer revolution invaded the world of Evangelical mission

---

1. One perspective on this: "… humans began animating inert objects with tiny slivers of intelligence, connecting them into a global field, and linking their own minds into a single thing. […] There is only one time in the history of each planet when its inhabitants first wire up its innumerable parts to make one large Machine. Later that Machine may run faster, but there is only one time when it is born. You and I are alive at this moment. […] This will be recognized as the largest, most complex, and most surprising event on the planet" (Kelly, 2005, p. 133).

2. Usually attributed to Mark Twain.

strategy, it brought in new tools, enormously helpful tools, for the tasks at hand. Here were nails sticking up, and, happily, hammers arrived. Then again, maybe these exciting new tools led Evangelical mission strategists to see the world in a different way, a less organic and more mechanical way, a less holistic and more divided way. Hammers arrived, and, unhappily, the world began to look like a bunch of nails.

World Vision and Campus Crusade for Christ were among the first American Christian organizations to use computers. They were applied to accounting, receipting, and other repetitive finance-related tasks. These mission organizations thus saved vast amounts of staff time and expense. Ed Dayton left his career in aeronautics engineering for missions, and became a key leader in World Vision, a leading Christian relief and development agency. When a computer arrived in the office, he wondered if this power to organize and present large masses of information could somehow be yoked to the global task of world evangelization. Thus MARC was born, the Missions Advanced Research and Communication center, as an entity within World Vision. Among other tasks, MARC set their computer to compiling the data for, or producing, ten editions of the *Mission Handbook*, the definitive directory and guide to the North American Protestant missions movement[1].

Dayton served on the Strategy Working Group that emerged from the 1974 Lausanne Congress on World Evangelization. This Group was quick to latch onto, and promote, the priority of reaching the world's unreached people groups, or the cause of Frontier Missions. In 1976 Ralph and Roberta Winter founded the US Center for World Mission (USCWM) in Pasadena, California, to also vigorously and extensively promote this cause. MARC started a database of unreached peoples, compiled from submissions sent in from near and far. From that they published a series of books, the Unreached Peoples annuals[2], seeking to identify and describe these peoples for prayer and evangelizing activity.

1. MARC compiled the data for the 8th, 9th, and 10th editions, and then both researched and produced the 11th to the 17th editions of the Mission Handbook. That last one was Siewert and Valdez (1997).

2. The first of the series was Unreached Peoples '79: The Challenge of the Church's Unfinished Business (Wagner & Dayton, 1978); the seventh and final was *Unreached Peoples: Clarifying the Task* (Schreck & Barrett, 1987).

David B. Barrett, an aeronautics engineer and test pilot in Britain, felt the 'call of God' to missionary service, left his career, studied theology and missions, and was sent to serve God in Kenya. Years later, he was working on the first edition of the *World Christian Encyclopedia* (Barrett, 1982). When Ed Dayton visited Barrett, Dayton saw the masses of information Barrett was compiling and organizing, and recognized this as a task crying out for computing power, so he helped Barrett acquire a minicomputer. Actually, computers were nothing new to Barrett, even then. Between 1946 and 1960 he published "*Missionary Notes*, a publication that applied scientific and aeronautical methodologies to mission, utilizing Britain's first operational computer, the electromechanical Colossus with its 18,000 vacuum tubes and covering some 2,000 square feet of floor space" (Bonk, 2007, p. 1). Before the W*orld Christian Encyclopedia* was published in 1982, Barrett's World Evangelization Research Center was extensively supported by database technology.

Patrick Johnstone, trained as a chemical engineer, became an itinerant missionary evangelist in southern Africa, and compiled the first global *Operation World* in Zimbabwe (then Rhodesia) while traveling and preaching[1] (Johnstone & Mandryk, 2001). Years later, when Johnstone was working from the WEC International headquarters near London, Ed Dayton helped him acquire a multi-user computer, which took its place at the center of the production of the 1986 edition (Johnstone,1986), an information-packed, thoroughly-researched guide to praying for every country in the world. Note that both of these enormously influential research products, the *World Christian Encyclopedia and Operation World*, were born in Africa.

Summer Institute of Linguistics (now SIL International, related to the organization Wycliffe Bible Translators), in their quest to see the Bible translated into every language on earth, entered the world of computers well before the personal computer (PC) revolution erupted. SIL collected a vast trove of detailed information on the world's languages, published in the series of *Ethnologues*

---

1. A short history of Operation World can be found in Johnstone and Mandryk (2001).

(Lewis, 2009[1]). Again, here was a mountain of names, alternative names, facts, statistics, and more that cried out for the organizing power of computer technology.

Jim Montgomery, a missionary with an organization, Overseas Crusades (now OC International or One Challenge), was one of the first students of Donald McGavran[2] in his nascent Institute of Church Growth, based in Eugene, Oregon. Montgomery, following the earlier work of Leonard Tuggy (1971), studied the growth of evangelical denominations in the Philippines, compiling facts and statistics at every turn. His work led to the development of the DAWN (Discipling A Whole Nation) idea, with its vision of a church, a living expression of the Body of Christ, in every community of the nation; such that everyone has a church they can get to (close enough in physical distance) and a church they would go to (close enough in cultural distance). This strategy called for extensive new church planting guided by detailed information on all the peoples and places of the diverse, complicated nation of the Philippines.

Montgomery eventually moved to the OC headquarters in San Jose, California, to become their director of research. Coincidentally, San Jose is in the heart of Silicon Valley, where the personal computer revolution was, at that time, exploding. Silicon Valley is an area near San Francisco that has been the birthplace of the vacuum-tube amplifier, Hewlett-Packard, radar, Fairchild Semiconductor, computer networking, Intel, the floppy disk, gene splicing, the Xerox Palo Alto Research Center (PARC), Apple Computers, relational database technology, Sun Microsystems, Silicon Graphics, Cisco Systems, Mosaic, Netscape, Yahoo!, and Google (Silicon Valley website[3]).

Bob Waymire was a hard-driving, fast-moving and ambitious rocket engineer for Lockheed. In this fast-paced life his marriage failed and he saw his life spiraling downward rapidly. His secretary, a committed Christian, cared and prayed for

---

1. Current edition.

2. Dr Donald MacGavran was a professor at Fuller Theological Seminary in Pasadena, USA and known in evangelical circles as the father of the Church Growth Movement.

3. Retrieved from www.netvalley.com/svhistory.html

him, and he was later converted to Christ. Soon after, he entered the missionary vocation. By the early 1980's Bob Waymire and Jim Montgomery together led the Research and Strategy Department of OC, and acquired a computer to help with DAWN-related research. Waymire attended a computer convention and for the first time in his life saw computer-generated maps, which displayed quantitative data linked to geographic locations. Waymire testifies to a powerful spiritual experience at that moment, walking and praying behind the booths at this high-tech convention, 'claiming' GIS (geographic information systems) for the cause of Jesus Christ.

Bill Dickson became a Christian in college while earning a degree in Electrical Engineering with concentrations in computer science and communication systems. He came home from the 1976 Urbana missionary convention discouraged that none of the scores of mission agencies represented had any idea what to do with an electrical or computer engineer. Dickson met Bob Coleman, a graduate of Cal Tech, the California Institute of Technology, one of the world's leading science and technology universities. Coleman was then serving as an assistant to Ralph Winter. When Dickson learned of the unreached peoples it seemed clear to him, "if you're dealing with thousands of anything, you've got to get a computer in there somewhere" (Dickson, personal communication, January 27, 2008). Coleman introduced Dickson to Waymire, which led to Dickson helping Waymire with technological tasks at the OC headquarters.

Pete Holzmann's father worked for General Electric, and Pete grew up in one of the few homes in the world at that time equipped with a computer teletype terminal. By the time he finished high school Pete had mastered a dozen programming languages. He had also made a firm decision to avoid computers, feeling they fostered unhealthy isolation. Later, as a student at Stanford University, needing money, he helped with certain well-paying computer tasks, and in the process found himself working with some of the world's leading computer experts.

At one point, Pete devoted his life to the Christian faith in a dynamic way, partly influenced by the tragic and untimely death of a Christian friend from high school. He graduated with a degree in semiconductor electronics, and discovered the only jobs he could get had to do with computers, even though he had a personal distaste for them. In time, he had a strong conviction that somehow God was saying to him, "I gave you this for a reason". After a time of prayer with his wife Leslie, in 1981 Holzmann became an independent consultant, to free up time for Christian lay ministry as a technologist. Soon, one 'high-tech' company agreed to pay him a full salary and cover all his work and travel expenses in exchange for one-quarter of his time. His feelings about computers changed. As he was helping to invent and maintain a new technology called 'email' he saw that computers could help, and not just hinder, human communication and interaction.

One day Holzmann was helping Dickson string network cables in the false ceiling of the OC headquarters building. Standing on a ladder, Holzmann was wondering to himself whether there might be any mission-related tasks that could make better use of his knowledge and skills than this simple chore. At that moment, Bob Waymire burst in, enthusiastically jabbering about what he had just seen of cutting-edge, sophisticated, computer-generated mapping and the potential it held for mission understanding, mobilization, and strategy. Holzmann responded, "It can't be that hard, really", and Bob Waymire, in his typical impulsive style, pointed his finger at Holzmann and bellowed, "This is going to happen, and *you're* the one who's going to do it!"

Holzmann gathered a group of friends, serious computer experts all, who worked for many months on what turned out to be a serious programming challenge. Their first triumph was a simple map of Guatemala, with data displayed by province, data related to the progress of evangelization and evangelical Christian presence. The base map was drawn with an early mouse pointing device that had a paper clip taped to it, and the programming and print-generating functions were similarly jerry-rigged. This humble map was in fact the first computer-generated, information-bearing map ever produced from the PC platform. In this case, and others, it was not a new technology shaping the Christian world mission, but the Christian world mission shaping the emergence of a new technology.

The moment he saw this humble map, Jim Montgomery was thrilled. Soon he boarded an airplane for Guatemala armed with a series of such maps, to promote the DAWN idea in that country. DAWN in time became a major force in the expansion of Evangelicalism in Guatemala, a process that eventually led to the election of an Evangelical (Efraín Ríos Montt) as President of the nation.

That Guatemala data came from the Global Research Database, or GRDb. Bob Waymire had asked permission to be released from OC for two years for a special project, to develop an extensive, comprehensive database of global missions-related information, linked to computerized mapping. In those heady early days of the PC revolution, Waymire expected that in the span of two years he could produce a database (the GRDb) that would contain and display dozens of categories of information on every country and people of the world, on the status of religion, Christianity, evangelization, and the like.

Bill Dickson had moved to Pasadena and was helping with technological tasks at the *US Center for World Mission* (USCWM). He had discovered there were mission agencies who desperately needed computer people, and computer people who desperately wanted to serve missions, but that the two would never find each other without some kind of intentional, visible structure. Thus in 1982, he formed *DataServe*. Ralph Winter, an engineer before he was a missionary, was himself a computer enthusiast. Bob Waymire moved to the USCWM in the summer of 1983, and Global Mapping Project (GMP; later Global Mapping International or GMI) was born there. In Pasadena Waymire found not only his former colleague Bill Dickson, but a group of technologically-astute Frontier-Missions zealots recruited from the *Cal Tech Christian Fellowship*.

Pete Holzmann balanced his time between serving as GMP's vice-president of research and development, and working with a commercial software company. In the latter role, he became the chief architect for the world's first PC-based geographic information system (GIS). Thus this significant technological development was largely crafted by a gifted brother who all along had in view its usefulness for world mission. The leading PC-based GIS software in the world today, ARC View, is the direct descendant of Holzmann's work. GMI's current

Global Ministry Mapping System, built on ARC View, is now being used by more than two hundred mission organizations around the world; about eighty of them are indigenous Indian missions.

Over time, the missiological perspective of GMP/GMI shifted. Their initial focus was on evangelization alone, from DAWN, Church Growth, and Frontier Missions thinking. In the late 1980s they joined with a zealous Norwegian missionary entrepreneur named Frank Kaleb Jansen, and with the missionary organization, *Youth With A Mission* (YWAM), to produce the book *Target Earth* (Jansen, 1989). Completed in 1989, in time for Lausanne II in Manila, it sold about 30,000 copies. *Target Earth* reflected a wide-ranging holism, drawing readers' attention not only to God's global concern for the lost, but also to his concern for the poor, the oppressed, the diseased, and the environment.

By the early 1990's, missionaries and national Christians in various places in the Majority World began applying the tools brought by the PC revolution to local, national, and regional mission research. Paul Hattaway, based in northern Thailand, has written many important books on China and Southeast Asia, some of which are products of his computer-based research, notably: *China's Unreached Cities, Vol. 1* (Hattaway, 1999a); *Faces of the Unreached in Laos* (Hattaway, 1999b); *Operation China: Introducing All the Peoples of China* (Hattaway, 2000); *China's Unreached Cities, Vol. 2* (Hattaway, 2003); and *Peoples of the Buddhist World* (Hattaway, 2004).

A missionary researcher in Asia who uses the name Omid, through brilliant, thorough, painstaking research, brought together a huge, detailed mass of information on communities and languages. Bob Waymire introduced him to computers. One database, on communities in South Asia, has 334,000 lines of data with about twenty-five fields of information per line. Another, on languages, has 545,000 lines of data, with about ten fields of information per line. Asian researchers also, with the help of computers, have produced such resources as *Unreached Mega Peoples of India* (Sathiaraj, 1999), *Operation Japan* (Mitsumori, Wright, & Cho, 2000), and *Indonesia's Unreached People Groups* (PJRN, 2003).

Thomas Wang was director of the Lausanne Committee for World Evangelization in the late 1980's. He and others noted the large number of significant Christian missions and denominations that were setting ambitious goals related to world evangelization by the year 2000 (Wang, 1987). Luis Bush, an Argentine, then president of Partners International, worked with Thomas Wang and others to plant seeds in Manila that blossomed into the founding of the AD2000 and Beyond Movement. Soon this ministry adopted the two-pronged goal of "A Church for Every People and the Gospel for Every Person by the Year 2000"[1] (Starling, 1981).

Luis Bush asked Pete Holzmann to help him better visualize and understand the global geography of the unreached peoples, the unevangelized, and human need. Using newly-released mapping software and data, Holzmann produced a series of maps that displayed, by country, such variables as religion, evangelization, and poverty. Bush was excited by these maps and the story they told. Better than ever before, he could clearly see and understand the wide swath of the Eastern Hemisphere where most of the world's non-Christians and unevangelized lived (and live). This belt extends across North Africa, much of the Middle East, Central Asia, much of South Asia, and parts of China and Southeast Asia. He defined this belt by latitude numbers, and spoke of the '10/40 Box' until his wife Doris got the idea in a prayer retreat that it should be a 'window,' like a window of opportunity for Jesus Christ. Thus the concept of the 10/40 Window was born. Bush wrote and published a full-color pamphlet, with five computer-generated maps, that enjoyed wide distribution and set a key term at the heart of Evangelical mission activity for the decade[2] (Bush, 1992).

Bush, who became the director of AD2000 and Beyond, insisted on a solid program of monitoring. How could progress toward the goal of "A Church for Every People" be measured? Ron Rowland, then head of SIL's strategic information office, was the founder and leader of an inter-mission ad-hoc group

---

1. The first half of this slogan, "A Church for Every People By the Year 2000," came from Edinburgh '80. See Starling (1981).

2. Maps by Pete Holzmann, unattributed.

called Peoples Information Network, or PIN. By 1994, PIN became a task force of AD2000 and Beyond. A draft book (Rowland,1995) was published for the AD2000-sponsored Global Consultation on World Evangelization in Seoul (GCOWE '95). This merged every major list of unreached peoples, or peoples that needed a church-planting movement if the goal of "A Church For Every People" was to be met.

The bad news is that this published list was so clogged with inaccuracies, duplications, omissions, and the like, that it was made useless. The good news is that it sparked new and better research. The Joshua Project was formed, as a ministry of AD2000 and Beyond. Dan Scribner, trained as a mechanical engineer, was introduced to the Frontier Missions vision, left his career, and joined the staff of the USCWM. Seconded to AD2000 and Beyond, he, together with Bill Morrison and others, leaped urgently into developing a viable unreached peoples database. They worked extensively with existing peoples and languages databases, received much help from Patrick Johnstone, and sought information from Christian workers in many countries. Luis Bush traveled to and fro around the world with printouts of people group lists tucked under his arm, for local leaders to add to, subtract from, and correct.

Soon, it was all refined down to a list of 1,539 groups, and countdowns began. By the time of the Amsterdam 2000 conference in July/August of that year, many unreached peoples still had no church-planting team present in their midst. Most of them, however, had at least been 'adopted' by one mission or another that promised to seek to reach them. Only 239 peoples remained 'unadopted' by any mission for church-planting ministry. As it turned out, top leaders of several major Evangelical agencies[1] found themselves together at "Table 71" at the conference, and agreed to move that number to zero. So at least that goal, to that extent, was reached by the set AD 2000 deadline. The Joshua Project database lives on. Scribner, Morrison, and their colleagues expanded it to assess all peoples of all countries and all sizes. In 2007 their

---

1. These included Campus Crusade for Christ, YWAM, Walk Thru The Bible, Intl. Mission Board (So. Baptist), DAWN Ministries, SIL/Wycliffe, and Mission Spokane. See www.table71.org.

website had 600,000 visits, 2.9 million page views, and about twenty thousand downloads of data.

The second edition of the *World Christian Encyclopedia*, published in 2001 (Barrett, Kurian, & Johnson, 2001), was largely built from a complex set of linked databases that each enhanced the usefulness and accuracy of the others. This set of databases, including ones on countries, religions, Christian churches and denominations, peoples, cities, provinces, languages, organizations, and bibliography, is now largely available on the Web as the World Christian Database.

Now many large, complex, mission-relevant databases are accessible on the Internet. Mapping capabilities figure prominently. A broader and more holistic vision of Christian missions is appearing, including through these websites:

- www.4kworldmap.com. A global plan of YWAM built around a detailed map that divides the world into about four thousand zones, with assessment of physical and spiritual needs in each.

- www.ethnologue.com. Global languages information from SIL International, with extensive bibliography.

- www.joshuaproject.net. Information on all ethnic peoples of the world, with loads of mission-related resources including profiles, pictures, stories, and links.

- www.missioninfobank.org. A collaborative missions library, database, and mapping site from Global Mapping International. In a way this represents the fulfillment of the old GRDb vision.

- www.peoplegroups.org. Contains religious and demographic information for ethno-linguistic peoples globally. From the International Mission Board (Southern Baptist).

- http://worldchristiandatabase.org. From the research of David Barrett, Todd Johnson, and Peter Crossing. Comprehensive statistical information on world religions, Christian denominations, countries, regions, people groups, cities, and provinces.

- www.worldmap.org. Country profiles and many maps, including Churches in Habitat information seeking to show the status of Evangelical church presence in all cities, towns, and villages, globally.

3. Evangelicals, tools and tasks

How then, does this story of Christian evangelicals inform the question of tools and tasks?

1. Whenever someone had the opportunity to computerize a mission research task, it seemed an easy decision. It would save much time, money, and knowledge. It would gain much efficiency, speed, accuracy, and power in analyzing, presenting, depicting, and communicating mission-relevant information. Good things were saved; good things were gained; were any good things lost?

On this point we have a debate. On the one hand, people like Schultze (2002) exhort:

"After admitting the 'lightness' of our digital being –its cosmic and moral shallowness– we should distrust the prevailing techno-magic that promises us inflated benefits from our use of cyber-technologies. We also need continually to [sic] de-technologize our religious traditions by ridding them of excessive technique and renewing their virtue-nurturing practices" (Schultze, 2002, p. 24).

On the other hand, consider the perspective of Nye (2006):

"Technology [...] is a fundamental human expression. [...] Cultures select and shape technologies, not the other way around [...]. For millennia, technology has been an essential part of the framework for imagining and moving into the future, but the specific technologies chosen have varied. [...] Each group of people selects a repertoire of techniques and devices to construct its world" (Nye, 2006, p. 210).

Nye (2006) sees that the varied cultures of the world remain varied partly because of their decisions about technologies, decisions that are instinctual or examined, but that very often prove to be creative and wise. People do not blindly choose the technologies they adopt.

2. Repeatedly in this story we came across Christians who (i) had technical expertise, and (ii) wanted to serve God in world mission. Should they have left their knowledge outside the gate, or did they do the right thing in bringing what gifts they had to the Church? Note this amazing convergence: Ed Dayton, David Barrett, Patrick Johnstone, Ralph Winter, Bob Waymire, Bill Dickson, Pete Holzmann, and Dan Scribner were all trained as engineers before they entered their missionary vocations. Would the world of Evangelical missions have been better off if all the engineers and technicians had been turned away at the door?

3. Rynkiewich (2007) has taken a direct shot at the people group approach to world evangelization, and by implication, at all the peoples-based, computerized research efforts described above. He wrote:

"There is an assumption here that the world is made up of discrete groups, and that persons have a clear-cut identity as a member of one or another of those groups. The world is not like that. It is questionable whether it was ever like that, except in the eyes of European explorers, missionaries, and 19th century anthropologists" (Rynkiewich, 2007, p. 224).

There is a powerful, maybe suspicious, convergence between the rise of the people group approach to world evangelization, and the rise of the powerful data-sorting and information-defining tool of PC-based databases. When the computer revolution was shaping the world, the people group approach was shaping Evangelical missions' understanding, mobilization, and action.

But then again, do none of the citizens of Fiji see themselves as ethnic Fijian, Hindi, Tamil, or Chinese? Do none of the citizens of Belgium ever talk about Flemish, Walloon, or German? Do none of the citizens of South Africa recognize any difference between Zulu, Xhosa, Swazi, Afrikaner, English, or Indian? Certainly the world missionary enterprise should work zealously toward racial and ethnic reconciliation, but in our present fallen world there is no sense in pretending these realities are only artificial outsider constructs, or imagining "the world is not like that". It was not a modern European or American who named categories of division when speaking of "every nation ... all tribes, and peoples, and languages" (Revelation, 7:9).

Thanks to globalization, in many places, ethnic identity and loyalty are growing weaker. Then again, in other places, ethnic identity and loyalty are growing stronger. A study of the Bible suggests that (and the wide experience of world mission confirms) God has created a world diverse in languages and peoples, all of whom will bring their praise to Him at the end of age. There are many cultures. There is more than one way to be human, and more than one way to be Christian.

4. Some rebuke the computer-based Evangelical mission research enterprise for setting the focus too much on evangelization alone. But is this critique against the use of computer technology itself, or against the missiological agenda to which the technology was applied? Current global mission research databases reflect a response to the wider range of human need. Computers are enormously flexible tools, as adaptable as they are powerful. As ministry perspectives moved, applications moved.

4.   Conclusion

The Internet and the computer revolution brought change. Not all change is evil. The technology of the printing press moved the church well away from earlier methods of evangelism, discipleship, teaching, and theologizing. The printed word became a tool of the Christian Church as well as a tool of the devil, spreading both truth and error as it was with the electronic word, the computer, the Internet, and all such media. The person who declares that computers take us a step away from being more authentically human or more faithfully Christian, must at the same time declare that the printing press also takes us a step away from being more authentically human or more faithfully Christian.

The power of technology need not be feared, but must be respected. When we are confronted with the next decision to computerize something, we do well not just to ask, "What can this do for us?" but also, "What will this do to us?"

References

Barrett, D. B. (1982). *World Christian encyclopedia: A comparative survey of churches and religions in the modern world, A.D. 1900-2000*. Nairobi: Oxford University Press.

Barrett, D. B., Kurian, G. T., & Johnson, T. M. (2001). *World Christian encyclopedia: A comparative survey of churches and religions in the modern world* (2 vols). New York: Oxford University Press.

Bonk, J. J. (2007). Movements, missiometrics, and world christianity. *International Bulletin of Missionary Research, 31*(1),1.

Bush, L. (n.d. ca. 1992). *The 10/40 window: Getting to the core of the core*. Colorado Springs, Colorado: AD2000 and Beyond Movement.

Hattaway, P. (1999a). *China's unreached cities* (Vol. 1). Chiang Mai: Asian Minorities Outreach.

Hattaway, P. (1999b). *Faces of the unreached in Laos: Southeast Asia's forgotten nation*. Chiang Mai: Asian Minorities Outreach.

Hattaway, P. (2000). *Operation China: Introducing all the peoples of China*. Pasadena, California: William Carey Library.

Hattaway, P. (2003). *China's unreached cities: A prayer guide for fifty of China's least evangelized cities*. Chiang Mai: Asia Harvest.

Hattaway, P. (2004). *Peoples of the Buddhist world: A Christian prayer guide*. Carlisle, UK: Piquant.

Jansen, F. K. (1989). *Target earth: The necessity of diversity in a holistic perspective on world mission*. Pasadena, California: Global Mapping International.

Johnstone, P. (1986). *Operation world: A day-to-day guide to praying for the world* (4th ed.). Bromley, England: STL Books.

Johnstone, P., & Mandryk, J. (2001). *Operation world: When we pray God works* (6th ed.). Cumbria, England: Paternoster.

Kelly, K. (2005, August 13). We are the Web. *Wired*. Retrieved from http://archive.wired.com/wired/archive/13.08/tech.html

Lewis, M. P. (Ed.) (2009). Ethnologue: Languages of the world (16th ed.). Dallas, Texas: SIL International.

Mitsumori, H., Wright, D., & Cho, Y. S. (2000). *Operation Japan: Japan in focus, a handbook for prayer*. Tokyo: Operation Japan Publishing Committee and Japan Evangelical Missionary Association.

Nye, D. E. (2006). *Technology matters: Questions to live with*. Cambridge, Massachusetts: MIT Press.

PJRN . (2003). *Indonesia's Unreached People Groups* [PJRN - Persekutuan Jaringan Riset Nasional]. Indonesia: Indonesian National Research Network.

Ramo, J. C. (1996, December 16). Finding God on the Web. *Time*. Retrieved from http://content.time.com/time/magazine/article/0,9171,985700,00.html

Rowland, R. (1995). *The least evangelized peoples of the world*. Dallas: Peoples Information Network.

Rynkiewich, M. A. (2007). Corporate metaphors and strategic thinking: The 10/40 Window in the American evangelical worldview. *Missiology, 35*(2), 217-241.

Sathiaraj, D. (1999). *Unreached Mega Peoples of India*. Chennai: India Missions Association.

Schreck, H., & Barrett, D. B. (Eds). (1987). *Unreached peoples: Clarifying the task*. Monrovia, CA: MARC and Birmingham: New Hope.

Schultze, Q. J. (2002). *Habits of the high-tech heart: Living virtuously in the information age*. Grand Rapids: Baker Academic.

Siewert, J. A., & Valdez, E. G. (Eds). (1997). *Mission handbook: U.S. and Canadian Christian ministries overseas, 1998-2000* (17th ed.). Monrovia, California: MARC.

Starling, A. (1981). *Seeds of promise: World consultation on frontier missions, Edinburgh '80*. Pasadena, California: William Carey Library.

Tuggy, A. L. (1971). *The Philippine church: Growth in a changing society*. Grand Rapids: Eerdmans.

Wagner, C. P., & Dayton, E. R. (Eds). (1978). *Unreached peoples '79: The challenge of the church's unfinished business*. Elgin, Illinois: David C. Cook.

Wang, T. (1987). By the year 2000: Is God trying to tell us something? *World Evangelization*.

5 Searching for French civilization: Reflections on situating information literacy skills in an undergraduate curriculum

Carmel O'Reilly[1]

*"I am other to myself precisely at the place
where I expect to be myself"* (Butler, 2004, p. 15)

Abstract

This chapter questions and reflects on the changing role of the foreign language and civilization lecturer as educator, when information literacy skills are situated in an undergraduate curriculum. As such, it does not set itself the task of providing solutions. Instead, it considers all the complications which occur en route to a greater use of Internet-based information sources within the discipline of French studies. In a departure from standard academic writing, I am inserting myself directly in the argument which follows a trajectory from my initial reluctance towards the Internet and the changes required of me in order to adapt. This chapter uses existing research to outline the current state of play regarding the digital debate within education. However, rather than reaching a specific conclusion, this chapter captures a recent moment of a situation in flux within higher education.

Keywords: information literacy, Internet and French civilization, Google and education.

1. E-mail address: carmel.oreilly@dit.ie

How to cite this chapter: O'Reilly, C. (2014). Searching for French civilization: Reflections on situating information literacy skills in an undergraduate curriculum. In J. D. James (Ed.), *The Internet and the Google age: Prospects and perils* (pp. 99-115). Dublin: Research-publishing.net. doi:10.14705/rpnet.2014.000180

1.   Introduction

In any debate, we are encouraged to take a position that is either for or against whatever may be under discussion. Of course, it is also possible to disengage from the discussion and take neither position. However, Butler (2004), in a series of essays, provides us with the possibility of yet another option. In her introduction, she explains that the experience of undoing restrictive conceptions of life can initiate relatively newer ones that have greater viability as their aim. Similarly, my own attempts to facilitate students' higher-level skills when using Internet sources, such as Google, for academic purposes, have caused me to undo restrictive notions of what it means to be a lecturer in higher education. Indeed, rather than adopt a position for or against the use of Internet-based information sources within the digital debate, these attempts are in the hope that a relatively newer role that has greater viability may be initiated. Like Butler (2004), my reflections on the experience of situating information literacy skills in an undergraduate French curriculum have revealed me to be "other to myself precisely at the place where I expect to be myself" (p. 15).

2.   Digital natives and digital immigrants

In their thought-provoking review of the digital debate, Bennett, Maton and Kervin (2008) discuss two important assertions: "(1) that a distinct generation of 'digital natives' exists; and (2) that education must fundamentally change to meet the needs of these 'digital natives'" (p. 777). We have become accustomed to the notion that there exists a generational divide among digital technology users. This may be attributed to the term "net generation" used to describe the generation born roughly between 1980 and 1994 and after (Tapscott, 1998). Prensky (2001a, 2001b) has given us the term "digital natives" to describe the same generation due to their knowledge and regular use of information and communication technology (ICT). However, current research suggests that it may well be the case that there is as much variation within the digital native generation as between the generations (Bennett et al., 2008, p. 779). Nonetheless, Coverdale (2013), a researcher and practitioner in educational technology, in a recent posting to his blog, warns against the current default position of "routinely rubbishing digital natives" while maintaining that "[i]t is only right that we continue to expose and challenge terms we believe to be erroneous" (para. 2, 9). Indeed, important questions have been raised about students' everyday ICT skills and their relationship to education. When it comes to assessing a website's suitability for an educational project, for example, existing research reports that students appear to adopt a "snatch and grab philosophy" or that they often make "hasty, random choices with little thought and evaluation" (Bennett et al., 2008, p. 781). The result is a "lack of critical thinking when using Internet-based information sources", which implies that "students aren't as net savvy as we might have assumed" (Bennett et al., 2008, p. 781). Based on existing research, it may be concluded that "education has a vitally important role in fostering information literacies that will support learning" (Bennett et al., 2008, p. 781).

In a kind of virtual echo of this call to action, Catherine Cronin, educator and academic coordinator of online Information Technology (IT) programs at the National University of Galway (Ireland), in a blog posting, outlines a series of challenges facing educators. Among them, she asks this question: "what are we doing to create or link to relevant online resources for students?" (Cronin, 2011, para. 5). While integrating information literacy skills into the civilization element of an undergraduate French curriculum seems like an appropriate answer, the question of exactly how to go about this still remains. In other words, while it is not difficult to give students a reason to use a search engine like Google in order to explore themes of French civilization, it is another matter entirely to consider how they are searching, or (re)searching, the Internet as an information resource. What emerges is an opportunity to extend traditional lecturing beyond the reach of text books into the World Wide Web in an attempt to foster information 'literacies' that will support learning. What follows fast on the heels of this exciting opportunity, however, are a number of difficult dilemmas. Let us first identify these dilemmas, and then consider them in the context of scholarly activity, and in light of existing research.

The integration of information literacy skills into the civilization element of the French undergraduate curriculum is part of the ongoing *Get Smart! initiative* at Dublin Institute of Technology (DIT) within the School of Hospitality Management and Tourism. The *Get Smart! initiative* uses a range of innovative learning and teaching interventions in an attempt to develop personal and professional skills in first year undergraduate students attending DIT (O'Rawe, 2010). One of the key elements of the initiative is the development of information literacy skills. Language education is an integrated component of undergraduate studies within the School of Hospitality Management and Tourism. Civilization studies are an element of the first year undergraduate French language modules. In a first assignment, students are required to search the Internet in order to answer questions about French current affairs, history, politics and culture. While there are marks for answering these questions correctly, a percentage of their overall mark in Civilization is attributed to how they have searched the Internet in terms of the webpage cited in support of their answers. Basic themes of culture and civilization are explored in class in the form of lectures supported by reading material and discussion. These include, for example, French identity, the geography and regional organization of France and the diversity of the French speaking world.

The first dilemma encountered involves the false assumption that all undergraduate students belong to the net generation. As such, they must be digital natives who require little, or no help, nor indeed teaching, when they are required to search the Internet in order to find information. It may as such be a case of misplaced instinct, as Coverdale (2013) suggests when he observes that "it seems digital natives 'took off' in wider academic (and non-academic) discourse because it tapped deeply into what seemed to instinctively describe significant differences in the emerging practices of digital technology users" (para. 4). As already indicated, we generally ascribe the notion, and indeed the term of digital natives, to Prensky (2001a). It is used to describe those born roughly after 1980. For those born prior to this time, which includes most teachers, Prensky (2001a) has introduced the term "digital immigrants" suggesting that the technological fluency of the former is almost alien to the latter. However, informal feedback from my own students suggests the absence of a single and distinct student body representative of a whole 'net' generation who can competently and confidently take control of the steering wheel when going on the Internet, as Tapscott (1998, p. 26) insists. Rather, what seems to emerge, is the "complexity of young people's computer use and skills" in keeping with existing research, the findings of which suggest "that technology skills and experience are far from universal among young people" (Bennett et al., 2008, pp. 777-778).

While some students in 2012 demonstrated good technology skills and experience, both in terms of finding the correct answer and accurately citing the website which they had consulted, a significant number seemed to be completely lost. This prompted a different approach the following year. Once a theme was explored in class, for example French identity, students were given three sample questions from the previous year's assignment in order to practice searching the Internet in advance of their assignment. The lecture and subsequent discussion covered topics such as the French national anthem, the French Revolution, French national symbols, their meaning and origins, and the French population and citizenship.

Example: digital narrative

These are an example of 3 sample questions, translated from the original French into English:

1. The famous French motto is Liberty, Equality, and Fraternity. One of these qualities has been personified in a famous painting. Find the title of this painting and the name of the painter.

2. What links Nicolas Luckner to the French national anthem?

3. A child born in France to two foreign parents does not have French nationality. However, this does not apply to a country with which France has historical ties. Name this country.

A small minority of students got all 3 answers correct; most succeeded in getting one or two correct; others got all 3 wrong. Indeed, as might be unexpected, some students claimed to be so daunted by the task that they attempted none of the 3 questions.

The answers were as follows:

1. 'La Liberté guidant le peuple' by Eugène Delacroix.
2. The French national anthem was dedicated to Nicolas Luckner.
3. Algeria.

Once the answers were delivered, a brief demonstration of how to go about a successful Internet search for these answers followed. Seeming a simple enough task, and indeed, a good idea at the time, the demonstration of how to conduct a successful scholarly Internet search proved challenging in more ways than one and not only for the students. Downes (2007) advocates using Google precisely because

> "a person using Google does not obtain information from a centralized source; rather, by typing a search term into the simple interface on the main page, users obtain information from anywhere around the world, from any of tens of millions of sources" (Downes, 2007, para. 4).

On the surface, this sounds exciting, useful and potentially helpful. However, Michael Gorman, when he was president-elect of the American Library Association, made a clear distinction between information and knowledge. He differentiates between information, which he describes as "data, facts, images, quotes and brief texts that can be used out of context" and recorded knowledge, which he claims to be "the cumulative exposition found in scholarly and literary texts" and which must always be taken in its context (Gorman, 2004, para. 6). In a follow up piece in the Library Journal, Gorman (2005) describes Google as a "notoriously inefficient search engine" providing thousands of 'hits' (which may or may not be relevant) in no very useful order" (para. 3).

Indeed, the class demonstration yielded so many choices that it was difficult to make a selection. When different search words were entered, a different set of options appeared. It was time consuming and even seemed to be time wasting. What was interesting was the number of enthusiastic, yet different, suggestions made by students, to either choose a site that they recognized had yielded the correct answer from their own search words, or to choose an entirely different site to see if that too yielded the correct answer. What was particularly challenging was the kind of chaos this created. There was a clear loss of control as I surfed my way from site to site, scrolling down, scrolling back up, opting for this link over that one, picking up speed in order to follow one link, then another, as the suggestions from students came rolling in and answers finally were found.

Gorman (2004) has received much attention for his distinction between information and knowledge, with one commentator claiming this to be "a reasonable, if pedestrian, observation" while also suggesting that it is "slightly nannyish advice", similar to, "be sure to eat your vegetables when you use Google" (Drum, 2004, para. 2, 3). However, it is Gorman (2004) who highlights the importance of speed over the time-consuming discernment of content in Google searches (para. 5). Then again, Gorman (2005) also maintains that the searcher obtains "heaps of irrelevance in nanoseconds" insisting that we be mindful of the fact that "rubbish is rubbish, no matter how speedily it is delivered" (para. 4). Certainly, the students wanted a fast, efficient search, which I must confess, the class demonstration did not deliver. Still, unlike Gorman's (2005) suggestion of "heaps of rubbish" (para. 4), the answers to the civilization questions were indeed there to be found. What is needed it seems, is the skill to better refine the search terms used. Also, a great deal of patience is required in order to read, discern and determine what may, or may not, be useful.

3.   The Google effect on research

Another dilemma occurs when we take into account that not only do different search terms yield different results, in terms of the listed resources available to explore, these listed resources are not fixed and so may also be subject to change. While Downes (2007) is critical of Gorman's (2004) dismissal of Google, precisely because it does not deliver well-ordered searches, he is willing to accept that Gorman's (2004) recommendation for libraries and librarians over digitized books is a modest one (para. 14). Nonetheless, Downes (2007) does highlight the 'constantly changing' nature of Google because "new resources arrive; new words produce new search results" (para. 9). What has proven to be a challenge for a class demonstration precisely because a site that was sourced in advance by a particular set of search words, may or may not yield the same results a week later, is for Downes (2007), a distinct advantage of Google. He observes that "it is not just a catalogue or index; it becomes, through its dynamic listing of resources, a way for people who don't know each other to communicate" (para. 9). Indeed, it seems that the dynamic and constantly changing nature of Google may even require communication in order to stabilize what appears to be the ever-shifting ground of information that it supplies.

Certainly, informal feedback from students prompted one to suggest that the class Facebook page might be used to post possible answers to the civilization questions which could then be further explored by others. Similarly, Cronin (2011) has highlighted 'open, participatory and social media among the challenges facing educators in terms of technology use. She suggests that "not all student work must be submitted directly and privately to the lecturer – opportunities for openness, sharing and collaboration should be considered" (Cronin, 2011, para. 6). Still, the teacher in all educators must surely wonder if that is not a lot like copying, while the explorer in every educator must surely wonder if it is not a really good idea! Somewhere between these two possibilities lies the truth of the matter. A little experimentation is required in order for us to decide. Mary Gallagher, an academic at University College Dublin and author of a most interesting analysis of Irish Higher Education, concedes that we need to understand more about the challenges and potential of digital technology in education. This includes, she advises, being "open to the palette of possibilities of new ways of being human, new ways of relating to each other and to the world and its diversity" (Gallagher, 2012, p. 225). She goes on to recommend that educationalists and educators in particular "need to be open to the promise of other kinds of attention than the deep and slow solitary attention and endurance required to read a book carefully, in depth and in detail, from end to end" (Gallagher, 2012, p. 225). Yet, she cautions that even so, they clearly need to adhere "to the importance of thoughtfulness and attentiveness; they need to remain true to deep thinking, thinking unafraid of complexity or of contradictions" (Gallagher, 2012, p. 225). Indeed, a certain degree of vigilance and endurance may suffice for us to remain true to core values in higher education while embracing the potential of Google.

A third and final dilemma arises when we consider what may be the emotional side of technology use by students in terms of their varying attitudes and dispositions. While existing research cited by Bennett et al. (2008) points to potential differences in skill associated with social, economic and cultural issues *vis-à-vis* specific disciplines of study, these areas are yet to be investigated comprehensively. Similarly, Bennett et al. (2008) insist that "not yet explored is the relationship between technology access, use and skill, and the attitudinal characteristics and dispositions commonly ascribed to the digital native generation" (p. 778). Informal feedback from students in terms of the civilization element of their first year assignment yielded a range of emotions, attitudes and dispositions. At one end of the spectrum, there was the feeling of pride that a student may be technologically adept at finding correct answers to specific questions about French culture. Curiously, some students reported a fun-family experience, availing of the help of parents or siblings, much like a treasure trail. However, others reported much impatience and frustration when answers were not found, or indeed, when searching provided what could be considered a false trail leading to wrong answers. Probing the matter with questions about how the search was conducted produced what appeared to be embarrassment, or perhaps guilt, maybe even shame, among those students who may not be as technologically adept at using the Internet as might be expected of them because of the associated implications of their digital native status. While these observations and reflections are informal, they seem to indicate the importance of further research into the attitudes and dispositions of young technology users in a scholarly context. Indeed, further research seems to be necessary in order to best situate information literacy skills in the undergraduate curriculum.

It is important to note that all students performed remarkably well in the civilization element of their first assignment which required them to search online for answers. This may or may not be attributed to the use of a class Facebook page which may or may not have been used to post answers which could then be shared by the group. Academically, this is difficult to track and assess. Furthermore, it raises the question as to whether the civilization assignment is a group project or one that is performed by individuals, which was originally the intention. This in turn raises the thorny issue of whether or not technologically adept students are doing the work, and leading the way, while less technologically adept students are carried by them rather than by themselves. The marking scheme is limited to correct answers and accurately cited relevant websites which contain the answers. The marking scheme does not allow for determining which students actually do the work. Indeed, many students made at least one reference to the online encyclopedia, Wikipedia. Some went so far as to cite Wikipedia almost entirely for their correct answers. Again, the marking scheme does not allow for specific websites, rather it allows for an accurate citation which yields the correct answer.

Downes (2007) makes a useful suggestion that may be applicable to this situation when he observers that 'content creation' is neither limited to YouTube for example, nor indeed is it limited to the writing of an article. Contrary to Gorman (2004), who considers Google search results to be un-ordered, Downes (2007) insists that "the content created by Google searches, which manifests itself most evidently as the ordering of search results, also results in a demographic trail" (para. 16). It may be interesting to consider such a trail as an accurate account of how students conducted their online searches.

The explorer in me is tempted to pursue this line of enquiry. However, the academic begins to protest because the integration of information literacy skills seems to invite the ever-encroaching roles of librarian, and IT expert, to come even closer to what is traditionally considered to be teaching territory. Rather than class-based learning about civilization themes, provided by an academic, it seems that the students must be facilitated in their own learning by a combination of academic, librarian, and IT roles, in order to search online in a scholarly way. Indeed, I seem to be "other to myself precisely at the place where I expect to be myself" (Butler, 2004, p. 15).

4.   Implications for education

Certainly, the situating of information literacy skills in the undergraduate curriculum has implications for educators. The question remains to what extent must education change in response to these implications. A literature review undertaken by the Higher Education Academy in the United Kingdom cites a number of relevant studies about the net generation and digital natives (Jones & Shao, 2011). For example, one of the studies from 2008 focused on the Google generation, that is, those born after 1993. It reported "that the information literacy of young people had not improved with wider access to technology" (cited in Jones & Shao, 2011, p. 17). Another study from 2010 argues "that although digital native students may feel comfortable in a digital immersed environment at home, they often lacked information literacy skills or understanding of issues such as plagiarism and copyright" (cited in Jones & Shao, 2011, p. 17). Nonetheless, some critics continue to insist that our contemporary educational system needs revamping so as to be more in tune with the corresponding changes in today's university students. For example, "[i]f you are an experienced teacher, you almost certainly have students filling up your classes who are, in many ways, different from those in the past. You probably feel a need, or some pressure, (and may have even started) to do something different for them" (Prensky, 2010, p. 5). Similarly, we may be advised that "a powerful force to change the university is the students. And sparks are flying today. A huge generational clash is emerging in our institutions" (Tapscott & Williams, 2010, p. 29, cited in Jones & Shao, 2011, p. 43).

Yet we may also be advised by Jones and Shao (2011) that "there is no evidence that there is a single new generation of young students entering higher education and the terms net generation and digital native do not capture the processes of change that are taking place" (para. 1). Indeed, there is much evidence in the above mentioned study to suggest that "the gap between students and their teachers is not fixed, nor is the gulf so large that it cannot be bridged" (Jones & Shao, 2011, para. 4). Jones and Shao (2011) go on to observe that the relationship between students and teachers is, for the most part, based on the "requirements teachers place upon their students to make use of new technologies and the way teachers integrate new technologies in their courses" (para. 4). Thus it seems reasonable to first identify where gaps exist between teachers and students, before attempting to make suitable changes in curriculum and teaching practice, in order for educators to respond appropriately to the development of information literacy.

But how do we identify the situation where gaps exist between teachers and students? The renowned educational philosopher, Maxine Greene, recommends something she calls "wide-awakeness":

> "Without the ability to think about yourself, to reflect on your life, there's really no awareness, no consciousness. Consciousness doesn't come automatically; it comes through being alive, awake, curious, and often furious" (cited in Teaching Wide-Awake, 2008, para. 2).

While it is always a pleasure as an educator to admit to feeling alive, awake and curious, it is with a certain amount of humility that I admit to feeling, at times, particularly furious in my attempts to integrate information literacy skills into the French undergraduate curriculum. It is reassuring to consider that this may well be part of the experience of making suitable changes in order to meet the needs of a younger generation of university students. Certainly, this experience involves opportunities. As with all opportunities, there are, of course, challenges and dilemmas which require responses. These responses in turn require regular review and revision. The experience becomes a process of exploration, experimentation, reflection and review which engages not only the student but the educator too.

An important observation from my own informal research is that a unified new generation of university students with identical skills in the use of technology simply does not exist. Indeed, this is part of what remains most challenging because, not only are there differences between generations, but also there are clear differences within the digital or net generation itself depending on technology user-skills, attitudes, dispositions and emotional responses. Furthermore, the inherent nature of Google is that it is constantly changing as new resources are added and others are temporarily unavailable or removed. Indeed, different search words may yield entirely different results so that what appears to be unavailable, or removed, may in fact be retrieved. A comparison could be made with a second civilization assignment which the same students were asked to do. This involved searching a civilization textbook in order to find answers to multiple-choice questions within a specific time frame. The students demonstrated a marked decrease in interest and engagement both in terms of correct answers and in terms of the number of questions left unanswered. This is difficult to interpret however. It may be because marks were so high in the first assignment, that there was little incentive to achieve the same in the second, as the overall mark involves an aggregate of the two. It may be the result of a false assumption that students require little or no help when retrieving information from a textbook. It may be neither of these and just a matter of the time constraint imposed exclusively on the textbook assignment. Indeed, it may be useful to consider a second assignment in which students also search for answers online but within a time constraint. What is certainly worthy of note is that there was a marked increase in student engagement where the assignment required them to search the Internet for answers.

What is also worthy of note is that an educator is not necessarily a librarian. Nor is an educator necessarily an IT expert. Yet the situating of information literacy skills in the undergraduate curriculum requires a re-evaluation of all three roles, educator or academic, librarian and IT expert, in order to better address the changing needs of contemporary university students. Needless to say, my own experience of undoing what it means to be an educator has required me to explore becoming something of a librarian and something of an IT facilitator. While "I am other to myself precisely at the place where I expect to be myself" (Butler, 2004, p. 15), the experience has not necessarily been a bad one. It is possible that the students found less information about French civilization from lectures, textbooks and class discussion. Rather, they explored the possibility of accurately finding such information on the Internet by using Google and citing the websites consulted as relevant sources. However, this hardly signals the end of books, libraries and librarians. Gorman's (2004) response to the possibility of vast databases of digitized whole books, including scholarly books, seems excessive. He suggests that these are "expensive exercises in futility based on the staggering notion that, for the first time in history, one form of communication (electronic) will supplant and obliterate all previous forms" (Gorman, 2004, para. 8).

5. Conclusion

There is a need to be cautious about "dismissive skepticism", or indeed, "uncritical advocacy" when it comes to deciding whether the phenomenon of digital natives is significant "and in what ways education might need to change to accommodate it" (Bennett et al., 2008, p. 783). Certain scholars, such as Prensky (2001a, 2001b), will continue to draw our attention to the inadequacy of our current educational system claiming that it is no longer equipped to meet the changing needs of the present generation of university students because they are digital natives with ready-to-go information literacy skills; many others, such as Jones and Shao (2011) will continue to de-bunk the notion of digital natives as a unified generation of young students entering the portals of universities and colleges.

While this chapter has not set itself the task of providing solutions to the ongoing digital debate or offering specific conclusions as to the role of the educator, it seems reasonable that Google, or other Internet-based information sources, are here to stay. For now, Google continues to be the first port of call for enquires made by students who have in their possession a state-of-the-art, hand-held, technology device which they want to use. That this is already something of a natural reflex for students, whether they are particularly good at using the Internet or not, causes me to agree with Bennett et al. (2008) when they conclude that education does indeed have a vitally important role to play in fostering "information literacies" that may support learning (p. 781). In terms of how educators might go about fostering information 'literacies', it seems not only reasonable, but also prudent, to first identify where gaps exist between teachers and students, before attempting to make suitable changes in curriculum and teaching practice. It is in this way, according to Jones and Shao (2011) that educators may respond appropriately to the development of information literacy (para. 1).

As much of the literature quoted in this chapter suggests, and which indeed my own informal feedback from students further supports, there is a range of technology skills and experience among young people (Bennett et al., 2008, pp. 777-778). Some students require help in order to initiate their research, such as deciding which search words to enter in the Google interface. Others need help in order to organize the results of multiple searches. And so it becomes a part of the role of educators to facilitate students' critical thinking so that they may differentiate between what is academically useful, and what is not. After all, it is Downes (2007) who highlights the morass of data available on the Internet while Gorman (2005) reminds us of the extent to which this may, or may not be relevant. This already constitutes a significant change in the role of the educator because it encroaches somewhat on the role of the librarian as knowledge provider and to an even greater extent, perhaps, on the role of the Information Technology specialist. The role of the educator is further changed with the introduction to the curriculum of open, participatory and social media, as Cronin (2011) recommends. While this requires some experimentation with an educator's digital identity, which in turn requires a certain willingness to experiment with the notion of educator in the first place, admittedly, once information literacy skills are incorporated in the curriculum, this seems like the obvious next step.

Unless there is a major breakthrough in terms of a publication that tells us definitively how we may use the World Wide Web for academic purposes, we may never know for sure. What is certain is that educators will continue to need ongoing research, both formal and informal, to inform the debate about the ways in which education may need to respond to new university students in terms of the use of Internet-based information sources. While this chapter cannot accurately predict what the role of the French language and civilization lecturer may look like in the future, it does suggest that a relatively newer role may be initiated. Indeed, a certain degree of vigilance and endurance may well be enough, as Gallagher (2012) recommends, in order for educators to remain true to the core values of higher education, such as deep thinking, while embracing the potential of Google (p. 225). The best way forward, therefore, would seem to be in a Maxine Greene state of "wide-awakeness" (cited in Teaching Wide-Awake, 2008, para. 1): feeling sometimes curious and other times furious while remaining aware of the digital debate. Similarly, Gallagher (2012) reminds us that "a searching uncertainty" is the hallmark of any student or teacher, indeed of any person (p. 212). In this way, situating information literacy skills in the undergraduate curriculum might involve a process of shifting and observing so that a relatively newer role for the educator that has greater viability may be initiated.

Meanwhile, French civilization continues to extend beyond the boundaries of books and classrooms into cyberspace where wide-awake students may continue to search with a measure of uncertainty for answers to their questions.

References

Bennett, S., Maton, K., & Kervin, L. (2008). The digital natives debate: A critical review of the evidence. *British Journal of Educational Technology, 39*(5), 775-786. doi:10.1111/j.1467-8535.2007.00793.x

Butler, J. (2004). *Undoing gender*. New York: Routledge.

Coverdale, A. (2013). That digital natives thing. *PhD Blog (dot) Net*. Retrieved from http://phdblog.net/that-digital-natives-thing/

Cronin, C. (2011). Distributed creativity: Open education and challenges for higher education. *catherinecronin*. Retrieved from https://catherinecronin.wordpress.com/2011/12/07/distributed-creativity/

Downes, S. (2007). Places to go: Google's search results for the net generation. *Innovate, 3*(4). Retrieved from http://www.academia.edu/2869023/Places_to_go_Googles_search_results_for_the_Net_generation

Drum, K. (2004, December 17). Google and the human spirit. *The Washington Monthly*. Retrieved from http://www.washingtonmonthly.com/archives/individual/2004_12/005344.php

Gallagher, M. (2012). *Academic Armageddon: An Irish requiem for higher education*. Dublin: The Liffey Press.

Gorman, M. (2004, December 17). Google and God's mind. *Los Angeles Times*. Retrieved from http://articles.latimes.com/2004/dec/17/opinion/oe-nugorman17

Gorman, M. (2005, February 15). Revenge of the blog people! *Library Journal*. Retrieved from http://lj.libraryjournal.com/2005/02/ljarchives/backtalk-revenge-of-the-blog-people/

Jones, C., & Shao, B. (2011). *The net generation and digital natives: Implications for higher education*. Higher Education Academy, York. Retrieved from http://oro.open.ac.uk/30014/1/Jones_and_Shao-Final.pdf

O'Rawe, M. (2010). *Get smart! An evaluation of an initiative in personal and professional development among first-year undergraduates*. Report submitted to Dublin Institute of Technology, Ireland. Retrieved from http://www.dit.ie/lttc/media/ditlttc/images/teachingfellowships/reportsteachingfellowships/Get%20Smartfinal%20report%20MaryO'Rawe.pdf

Prensky, M. (2001a). 'Digital natives, digital immigrants part 1. *On The Horizon, 9*(5), 1-6. doi:10.1108/10748120110424816

Prensky, M. (2001b). Digital natives, digital immigrants part 2: Do they really think differently? *On The Horizon, 9*(6), 1-6. doi:10.1108/10748120110424843

Prensky, M. (2010). *Teaching digital natives: Partnering for real learning* (1st ed.). Thousand Oaks, CA: Corwin Press.

Tapscott, D. (1998). *Growing up digital: The rise of the net generation*. New York: McGraw-Hill.

Tapscott, D., & Williams, A. D. (2010). Innovating the 21st century university: It's time. *Educause Review, 45*(1), 17-29.

Teaching Wide-Awake. (2008, October 14). *Wide-awakeness*. Retrieved from http://teachingwideawake.wordpress.com/tag/maxine-greene/

6 Purposeful searching: Training students in Internet literacy for Italian studies

Etáin Watson[1]

Abstract

In this fast-changing information age, teachers and students can feast at a banquet of material on the Internet. This is a very good thing in these tight economic times, when education systems are strapped for cash and many arts and music courses are being cut in favor of classes to develop so-called marketable skills, such as business, biology or chemistry. So, teachers of language and language arts often try to find materials on the Internet to excite their students' interest. In this study, which reveals a teaching-learning approach, the students from the Dublin Institute of Technology in Ireland created their own virtual language environment as the teacher guided the students to search for resources on the Internet. In order to make the most of student time, I provided initial guidelines to help the students get good materials. First I taught them how to discriminate among sources, filter search results and document sources.

Keywords: Internet search, Italian studies, language learning, action research.

1.   Introduction

As a teacher in the 21st century, I have found it nearly impossible to teach satisfactorily using only the textbook in this age of immediate feedback, instant satisfaction, and short attention spans. Student engagement is so important that

1. E-mail address: Etain.watson@dit.ie

How to cite this chapter: Watson, E. (2014). Purposeful searching: Training students in Internet literacy for Italian studies. In J. D. James (Ed.), *The Internet and the Google age: Prospects and perils* (pp. 117-132). Dublin: Research-publishing.net. doi:10.14705/rpnet.2014.000181

the new media must be used in order to hold students' attention. I found that the best materials for post-secondary Italian language students were either movies or materials found on the Internet. The materials available on the Internet are just as useful as books, and more up-to-date, because the lag time in releasing published textbooks is months at best. Since the most commonly used vocabulary can be found in popular reading material, it makes sense to let students pick their own study materials. I also encourage the students to participate in role playing games, especially those games that have live sound. Most importantly, these up-to-date materials contain current cultural situations, which are critical for language learning (Omer & Ali, 2011).

Whereas teachers cannot do individual lessons for each student from a different source, it is possible to train the students to do their own (Gee, 2004). And to assess their learning, creating lessons, assessments and applying them can as easily be done by students with a good teacher's guidance (Gee, 2004). One might assume that to create lessons and assessments for students amounts to a great deal more work for the teacher, but such is not the case. The teacher's role becomes more like that of a mentor, which has inherent benefits for both parties.

It takes a bit more up-front planning to use this method, but the results are worthwhile. Basically we are teaching students to learn as a life-long process. Though some research shows that lecturers do not consider teaching students to learn as part of their jobs at post-secondary level, it is often necessary (Waeytens & Others, 1997). Students become self-disciplined self-educators once they have the tools required to make this transition (Cherif et al., 2009, p. 346). It is quite well documented that cooperative collaboration is a key element to active learning (Istifci & Kaya, 2011, p. 88). This approach empowers students to take charge of their own education, which is right in line with Gee's three necessities for learning: "Empowered learners, Problem solving, and Understanding" (2005, p. 6).

In this chapter I describe how to help students find relevant Internet materials that they like. In two separate classes, one ab-initio Italian and one intermediate

Italian, students were given a lesson on Internet media literacy. I presented them with the directions for conducting useful searches, including creating search strings, sifting the results, and using various resources on the Internet, such as search engines, compilation and review sites, social media and reference sites. Even Wikipedia can be useful in the beginning stages. Then I asked the students to find Italian folk tales in Italian and in English translation. The advanced students were asked to try doing their searches in Italian first, or to work in pairs with one searching in Italian and one searching in English. Computers were used in the school library and navigation tracking was turned on when they searched in order to record information that would help me to work with students to improve these results. At the suggestion of some advanced students, I added role playing games to the list of possibly helpful materials[1].

The students appreciated their training and they dug up some really interesting, culturally significant materials, such as cooking videos of Italian chefs, Italian street talk, and even a range of Italian folk tales. Using some ideas from Gee (2005), the students created some very interesting materials and assessments. The Internet is a banquet that can easily lead to information overload, but with some training and care, students can learn to navigate and benefit from their searching.

2.   Action research project

The teaching-learning approach I have proposed closely resembles an ongoing action research project (Stringer, 2007). In the case used for this study, there are two things that change the traditional curriculum and methodology of teaching: 1) environmental changes that modify what students will need for employment and life skills and 2) student performance and feedback.

---

1. Materials were basically reusable materials, often called reusable learning objects, such as PowerPoints, handouts, model lessons, templates for student group work, sample feedback for other students to use to critique other groups, plus copies of the lessons students created, which can be used both as real lessons and as models for future classes (Barritt, Lewis, & Wieseler, 1999).

The assessments at the end of the term are seriously considered in creating lessons and devising teaching methods for the following term. Student performance helps validate the methods used, as assessments are carefully segmented so that they can easily be attached to the teaching methodology and materials.

Action research, as defined by Stringer (2007), is a continuing cycle of "creation – presentation – assessment" (p. 19). So the methods and materials used this school term may change in the next term by being modified to better serve student needs. If students do not learn well with certain types of teaching methods (as was the case with my students), other methods will be devised until one works. If the students do not engage with the materials, then they are changed. This is ongoing and it is expected that it will continue, until the results are satisfactory. The biggest bonus in this type of teaching will come in the form of student involvement, because they are picking their own materials.

The project based upon this method used two classes of Italian for students at post-secondary level in Ireland. In this case, it was one class of mixed continuing education students from varied disciplines at intermediate level and one class of culinary arts students taking ab-initio Italian. The gender balance in the general class was 60 percent female, 40 percent male, and the culinary arts class was just the opposite. All students were aged 17-26. The average socio-economic status of students was lower-middle income and middle class. Their choice of Italian as an elective was based upon its connection to culinary arts or to the students' perception that it was an easy option. The project was conducted in semester one in 2011 and semester two in 2012. Seventy percent of students continued to the second year.

3.   Curriculum planning

3.1.   Outline of lessons

Depending upon the frequency of classes, these types of lessons can be used weekly or more often, as the teacher decides. In this case, the intermediate level met twice weekly and the beginner level met thrice weekly. One class was totally devoted to this project weekly with ten to fifteen minute periods as needed on other days.

3.1.1. Lesson one: introduction to research

- **Objectives**. The main objectives for this lesson are:

    1. to introduce the teaching methods;

    2. to create balanced groups. The pretest will allow the teacher to select at least one strong student and one weak student for each group so that no single group will have only strong or only weak students;

    3. to introduce Internet search methods, which will be detailed step by step on a handout, to aid students in finding what they need.

- The teacher provides a broad overview and description of what students will learn and how this will be accomplished (10 minutes). PowerPoint works well, but discussion is critical to get students involved right away. Offer this approach as an alternative and see if enough interest is stirred.

- The teacher pretests students to help create balanced student groups (10 minutes) and uses simple things like simple Italian cognates with English similarities, examples of simple grammatical concepts followed by multiple choice questions for correct Italian. Five to ten questions should give a broad range of innate ability.

- The teacher introduces research on the Web (20 minutes). The teacher will use multimedia setup or a laptop and projector to demonstrate. Search terms are discussed and some relevant strategies are introduced. In my Culinary Arts class, the demonstration included a failed search in English on Italian cooking, which brought up recipes in English. The better way to search, it was shown, is to change the search engine to Italian first, by entering http://www.google.it, and then commence the search on culinary arts. Even so, it was discovered that most results are still in English. Finally, using Google Translate, the teacher shows how to enter the Italian word for what the students want: *arti culinarie*. This brings up all results in Italian, even in the English search engine. Students can then use Google Translate to get an approximation of the translation.

First assignment. Student groups are directed to find an article written in the Italian language, summarize it briefly and rate it for interest, information and the trustworthiness of the source on a scale ranging from 1 to 5. The teacher then discusses with the class the criteria for the article and its assessment. Citations in simple APA style are required. The students in these classes were also told that student names should be included in parentheses for anything they create, so that the teacher can easily identify students' work. After a short time, student voices became discernible and one group was warned that all students needed to participate equally when the teacher realized that most of the writing was being done by only two members of the group. The classes were then reminded that class presentations and lesson delivery would be done as a group, with each student playing an active role. The review can be done in English and then be translated using Google Translate. Students are asked to list the useful vocabulary words within the article. Students were told they could use Google Translate, but that they should check the translation against their textbooks.

This plan was used for both classes in order to accommodate new intermediate students and to gently establish a routine for the term. Students were divided into groups so they could share and cooperate. They were advised to read the week's lesson and work on the vocabulary and could use the school library or the computer lab to access the Internet if they had no access at home. In addition, the researcher-teacher acquired several older laptops that were used for group work during class, one for each group. Grayford (1989) suggests that "structured" group learning activities, that is group work with definite guidelines and teacher monitoring, promotes a number of useful skills, including cooperation, leadership and negotiation.

3.1.2. Lesson two: using search engines and selecting reading materials

- **Objective**. The objective of this lesson is to connect what was learned from the first lesson to a new set of learning issues.

- Using PowerPoint plus projection of a live browser, the teacher demonstrates search engine strategies:

  - The students are required to figure out (Italian) words from the week's vocabulary lesson or from words learned so far, that could be of value to the student group. The teacher might use some vocabulary words in a sentence.

  - The students are asked to enter the least used word in common conversation or print (in their opinion) into the search engine first followed by the second and third least popular. For example, in English, if you want information about the best professional cooktop and oven you would use "cooktop", because it is seldom used for home ranges. By using quotation marks, the search engine is directed to find only the combination within the quotes, so the search for the best professional cooktop and oven would be written as: "cooktop and oven". This eliminates many possibilities. In the above case, adding professional will narrow results further.

  - The students are asked to either search these words or add one or two more key words. Google, and most other search engines, will search the first word you list and then search within the results sequentially on each of the rest.

  - Specify Web, video, image or whatever you want to see.

- Scroll through results and check out those that look interesting. Use Google Translate to read a bit of those that are under consideration. Meet with group, or call the other members to discuss possibilities or email them around until there is a consensus.

- The criteria for selection for this teacher-researcher's Italian Language classes are:

  - written in Italian;

  - between 300 and 1000 words, but complete, so it must not be a long article, but it can be a section of a longer article if it has a complete idea. One example might be something on training your dog and part one would be how to use commands. Subsequent parts may be used for future projects, if desired;

  - not overloaded with profanity;

  - uses at least 6-10 of the vocabulary words.

- The students are asked to copy the text and the link for citation (explain briefly why a citation is necessary). Note what search string was used.

The teacher uses the remainder of the class to talk about what students found. The teacher projects the URL on the screen and goes to the source. The class discusses the pros and cons of the choices. If the choice features all of the stated criteria, the teacher commends the student on the choice (the Culinary arts students used a lot of recipes and cooking videos).

Most students came back with very short items, but that was acceptable. The required vocabulary words were included in the first few assignments, because the most used words are those that they need to learn. At this point, I noticed that interest was waning, so I assembled the groups for the last ten minutes of class in order to introduce the next phase. The students compared what they had found and decided which they would do first. The groups identified vocabulary words and portioned out the translation of the agreed upon text. Students were also assigned a short exercise from the textbook. This was explained as necessary, since the book was useful for this practice and as a resource. It was mentioned that the book might have some phrases that would be useful for search strings in finding interesting parallel materials and it certainly provided vocabulary words.

3.1.3.   Lesson three: how to create learning materials

Class began with exchanged homework correction, and this was collected. A visual vocabulary warm-up was used for five minutes; the teacher intentionally used some humorous materials. This class was used for very detailed learning materials creation demonstration. The workshop format was used with the entire class. First what must be learned (task analysis) was introduced (Jonassen, Tessmer, & Hannum, 1999). Then the teacher and students connected this to how it can be learned by discussing learning styles and methods. Finally, these were connected to assessment, and the value of pre-assessment and post-assessment was discussed.

Once a useful task analysis was set, such as vocabulary, grammar elements, pronunciation and syntax, the students were led in a discussion of how these tasks might be accomplished. These were written on the whiteboard for reference. The teacher then showed different types of learning materials to find out what the groups of students liked to do. The task analysis was connected to the lesson plan and learning materials (Jonassen, 2004). Students discussed what they would learn by doing different things with the chosen material. Once everyone understood, then the students broke into groups to choose one or more lesson plans to create. Generally, students will need at least three types of learning materials to accomplish the various tasks in learning the language elements presented. It was felt necessary to discuss how to create matching assessments, both pre-assessment and post-assessment (Jonassen, 2004). Handouts had been prepared that included all these details for student information.

Teachers should be as interactive with the class as possible and reward close guesses with positive feedback. Any word or phrase that uses the proper rules also counts as a close guess. An example in English might be if an EFL student created a new word using the proper rules, such as "dividedly" for "separately". In Italian some students tried taking English words and matching them with familiar Italian words and the teacher added points. Other students grabbed what they thought were Latin roots and tried them. Basically, participation should be rewarded at this point.

The teacher demonstrated the creation of word matches in several forms using connected words, words and pictures, including several words that use different and matching cognates. The class created six good lesson examples during one period, and more than half the vocabulary for the lesson and all the grammatical concepts were introduced during the session. The corrected translated articles from each group were used.

The teacher used the last six minutes of class to show how to use Google Translate to help:

- put in one word and translate;

- put in second word and translate;

- put in the two words together and translate;

- check the dictionary. Some translations are quite funny, Google is fairly good but not perfect.

Assignment. The teacher directs students to come to class prepared with a short lesson to work within their groups. By this time in this particular case, each group had developed a dynamic for working and leaders had emerged. However, with the requirement that each time written work was turned in or presented to the class, the individuals within the group who created each part were acknowledged in a reduced method of citation developed for these classes, with just the student's name in parentheses following a segment. The groups had already selected their preferred article (with citation). Group translations were turned in. A second short exercise from the text was assigned. Some of the discussions about word meanings were quite interesting, as they involved cognates in English, but also the Italian context.

3.1.4. Lesson four: group lesson creation

The class was organized into groups right away. Corrected translations were passed out plus a copy of the entire correct translation. Groups were instructed to decide upon and create one grammar lesson and one vocabulary lesson based upon the current lesson requirements in the textbook using their work. The researcher observed each group and used the last ten minutes of class to get oral reports on progress from each group.

Assignment. The teacher directs student groups to finish creating two lessons and be prepared to present them to the whole class. These lessons were projected, discussed, corrected, and then done as a class, with the creating group moderating. Students were introduced to simple Italian phrases for correction and discussion and these were passed out in printed form.

Since the class had five groups, one or two of these class activities had to be used on a subsequent day. The presenting group received feedback forms from the rest of the class to help them improve. These were based upon a short printed template distributed to the class. Student feedback did not affect the grades. This tended to create an environment of class cooperation, and even negative feedback took a positive form as directed on the handout. It is believed that positive peer feedback, even when critical of the work, raises the self-esteem of both parties (Brookhart, 2011; Lipnevich & Smith, 2009).

The teacher distributes the corrected copies of each lesson that were printed and passed out for written homework exercises: these were easy but reinforcing. Student groups were assigned another document, plus a very short exercise from the book. The students were informed that much more Italian was expected in the assessments, and gradually they reached 100 percent Italian and improved in quality.

3.1.5. *Lessons five through ten*

For the next five lessons the above steps were repeated with new content. All lessons from the unit were completed in class or as homework. A brief unit exam was given. The teacher explained that due to her grading criteria the students would be allowed to eliminate the two worst exam scores from grading at the end of the term, with the exception of the mid-term and the final exam. With each subsequent lesson more and more Italian was used in class. By mid-term almost all the speaking in class was in Italian.

3.2.   The term length

Different school systems have a different number of weeks in the term, and there may be more or fewer classes per week than in this case study. The nature of this project is such that it caters for these differences. Because there was a need for a midterm exam and a semester final exam, two classes were devoted to these. In addition, students were given a group project lesson to complete with introduction, lesson, criteria and assessment. The final term grade for each group applied to all group members as part of their final grade. They all seemed to have fun with this, and some of the lessons were a bit playful but still valid.

3.3.   Assessment

Assessment can be done in a flexible manner. The researcher assessed the group work as one third of the grade, individual work as another third with the combination of the average of the quizzes after the two worst were removed, and the mid-term and final exams as the final third of the grade. Students understood this grading method and were comfortable with it. With group work worth one third, it has value because it will not unduly destroy a grade. In this manner, those students who perform very poorly in exams can still get an average grade, as can shy students.

3.4. Results

After these two groups were taught using the new framework, the need-to-repeat exams dropped by more than 20 percent. It was still necessary to do two weeks of review beginning in the second year, but more than 80 percent of students in each class had achieved a 65 percent score or better. Scores above the 90 percent mark rose very slightly and scores above 80 percent rose by about 10 percent. The class average was 74 percent for the beginners and 78 percent for the intermediate level.

3.5. Student feedback

Students were asked to rate their level of interest during the term on a scale of 1-5 with 5 being the highest score. The average rate of interest was 4.2, which is .4 higher than other classes at the same level during previous years. The school administration felt that the use of very interesting materials, besides the textbook, made all the difference. By comparison, the students who learned using classical Italian movies scored their interest almost as high, (4.0) but their grades were not quite as high and a slightly higher percentage of students had to retake the final exam to get a passing grade. Feedback from students indicated a rise in their confidence levels and enrollment in the second year class was higher than previous years by a small margin, though this cannot be solely attributed to the 'teaching to learn' methodology.

Students indicated that they enjoyed the classes more using this method rather than just using textbooks, ordinary homework, class drills and exams. About one third of the students mentioned that group work helped them learn, because the group members cooperated in sharing knowledge and ideas.

The students did not mention that they had, effectively, learned a little of how to teach when they created their lessons and then directed a class with what they had created. However, teaching was actually what they were doing at the time. Some students mentioned that they had learned a great deal about how to learn. This rather supports the theory that teaching is the best way to learn (Gartner,

Kohler, & Riessman, 1971). More than 80 percent of students said that finding their own materials was far more interesting than mere reliance on content in the textbook. Surprisingly, even students who had to retake the final exam indicated increased satisfaction and confidence.

It was noted that students were successfully engaged in the learning process and took an active part in creating and delivering the group lessons. After the first, somewhat tentative lessons were given by student groups, some of the groups became quite creative in how they 'taught' and they automatically explained why they did things the way they did in order to explain their own thinking.

It was evident by the time the third set of lessons was created that students were actually enjoying this process. A great deal of humor crept in as the term progressed. One lesson delivery included a short set of videos that the students created with free online cartoon software. The student showed an action and then spoke clearly in Italian about what the character was doing. She deliberately made a very wrong statement at one point and waited for the first objection. She then said, "I would give you extra points for listening". That increased student attention. Other students included jokes and word play games. It was evident that students liked 'playing' with the language.

4.   Discussion and conclusions

From this research program, it is apparent that increasing student engagement increases participation and assessment levels. From the teacher's observation, students were very interested in participating and assessment levels did rise from previous years with the same type of groups and when compared with other groups. Also, students were more engaged most of the time. Time allocation was an early problem, but the plans were adjusted to eliminate the issues. Homework levels increased as the term progressed and the use of Italian in class also increased. By the second term classes were conducted more than 90 percent in Italian.

Since the students' pass rate went up, it is assumed that this method had a positive effect upon students. It required slightly more work for the teacher at the beginning and required a more complicated assessment, but after the first three weeks, the teacher's workload was a bit less than usual, and classes seemed more productive.

The students liked using material they found and were quite interested in what other groups found. There were also lively discussions about what kinds of lessons worked best and which types of assessments actually showed progress. As the students learned about teaching, they invariably also learned about learning.

References

Barritt, C., Lewis, D., & Wieseler, W. (1999). *Cisco systems reusable information object strategy: Definition, creation overview, and guidelines. Cisco Systems.* Retrieved from http://www.ditausers.org/history/CiscoClarkRIO.pdf

Brookhart, S. M. (2011). Tailoring feedback: Effective feedback should be adjusted depending on the needs of the learner. *Education Digest, 76*(9), 33-36.

Cherif, A. H. Michel, L., Movahedzadeh, F., Aron, R., Adams, G., & Jenkins, S. (2009). Defending the lowly prokaryotes: New challenges for BIOGaia learning activity. *American Biology Teacher (National Association Of Biology Teachers), 71*(6), 346-353. doi:10.1662/005.071.0606

Gartner, A., Kohler, M. C., & Riessman, F. (1971). *Children teach children: Learning by teaching.* New York: Harper & Row.

Gee, J. P. (2004). *Situated language and learning: A critique of traditional schooling.* London: Routledge.

Gee, J. P. (2005). Learning by design: Good video games as learning machines. *E-Learning, 2*(1), 5-16. doi:10.2304/elea.2005.2.1.5

Grayford, C. (1989). A contribution to a methodology for teaching and assessment of group problem solving in biology among 15-year old pupils. *Journal of Biological Education, 23*(3), 193-198. doi:10.1080/00219266.1989.9655067

Istifci, I., & Kaya, Z. (2011). Collaborative learning in teaching a second language through the internet. *Turkish Online Journal of Distance Education, 11*(3), 88-96.

Jonassen, D. H. (2004). (Ed.). *Learning to solve problems: An instructional design guide*. San Francisco: Pfeiffer.

Jonassen, D. H., Tessmer, M., & Hannum, W. H. (1999). *Task analysis methods for instructional design*. Mahwah, NJ: Lawrence Erlbaum Associates.

Lipnevich, A. A., & Smith, J. K. (2009). I really need feedback to learn: Students' perspectives on the effectiveness of the differential feedback messages. *Educational Assessment, Evaluation and Accountability, 21*(4), 347-367. doi:10.1007/s11092-009-9082-2

Omer, K., & Ali, D. (2011). The Effect of culture integrated language courses on foreign language education. *US-China Education Review, 8*(3), 257-263.

Stringer, E. T. (2007). *Action research*. Thousand Oaks, California: Sage Publications.

Waeytens, K., & Others. (1997). Learning to learn: How do teachers differ? *ERIC (ED407385)*. Retrieved from http://files.eric.ed.gov/fulltext/ED407385.pdf

7 Symbolic instruments and the Internet mediation of knowledge and expertise[1]

Nicola F. Johnson[2]

Abstract

In this chapter, I demonstrate how Bourdieu's (1991) notion of symbolic instruments, that is structured and structuring structures, can be applied to the Internet to demonstrate the mediation and construction of knowledge and validation of expertise. This qualitative pilot study explored the online language and interrelationship between expertise, authority and constructions of knowledge. The structuring structures of five technology-focused websites are mapped in order to convey how the structured structures of online discourse mediate knowledge and expertise. The portrayal and authorization of 'experts' within these online forums help to shape the way that knowledge is constructed, contested and shared in the twenty-first century. This article extends Bourdieu's (1990) theory of practice in two ways: (1) arguing that the Internet is a field comprised of many sub-fields, and (2) identifying some of the symbolic instruments that structure and are structuring knowledge and expertise via social media available on the Internet.

Keywords: Bourdieu, symbolic, internet, expertise, structuring, structures.

1. A version of this paper was published in Continuum: Journal of Media & Cultural Studies, 2014, 28(3), 371-382 and is reprinted with amendments with the kind permission of the Editor, Panizza Allmark.

2. E-mail address: Nicola.johnson@federation.edu.au

How to cite this chapter: Johnson, N. F. (2014). Symbolic instruments and the Internet mediation of knowledge and expertise. In J. D. James (Ed.), *The Internet and the Google age: Prospects and perils* (pp. 133-152). Dublin: Research-publishing.net. doi:10.14705/rpnet.2014.000182

1. Introduction

While recent attention has been placed on collecting data from online forums (e.g. Loveland & Popescu, 2011; Vromen, 2011), focus is needed to explore the social process of attributing expertise (Collins & Evans, 2007) made by multiple Internet users. This project specifically focused on how active Internet users negotiate, construct and challenge knowledge and validate expertise. The purpose of this research was to document how people are constructing knowledge when they engage within and as part of online communities. This chapter reports on a recent study which conducted its research online via archival data collection in the form of observing the online from the offline (researcher as observer), that is, an ethnographic influenced approach.

The research question that this chapter focuses on answering is: how can we describe the online discourse used to negotiate and construct knowledge and expertise? This chapter details how active Internet users are validating knowledge and expertise via structuring structures independently constructed as part of a small number of online communities. These social practices construct authoritative knowledge and expertise only made possible via the user-generated nature of social media, namely Web 2.0 (for example, previously in the first version of the Internet Web 1.0, only those with computer programming knowledge could build and modify content on the Internet). User-generated content through the likes of blogs, wikis and social networking sites (which is what comprises Web 2.0) has meant that not only can more people participate in what goes 'on' the Internet, but also the ease of participation and the ubiquity of access have meant that the number of participants has exponentially increased (though not without its complications, see Kahne, Middaugh, Lee, & Feezell, 2012; Tacchi, 2012). The use of the Internet and its Web 2.0 features available via social media can be considered a social practice of mediated action within our particular historical moment and material space that is a site of engagement. Scollon and Scollon (2004) introduced the notion of *nexus analysis* which they claim

> "entails not only a close, empirical examination of the moment under analysis but also an historical analysis of these trajectories or discourse

cycles that intersect in that moment as well as an analysis of the anticipations that are opened up by the social actions taken in that moment" (p. 8).

Scollon and Scollon (2004) claim that a "social action taken repeatedly is considered a *social practice*" (p. 12). The regularity of access, postings and negotiation of social media means that this social practice is undertaken globally and daily by millions of people throughout the world.

This chapter provides some insight as to how technology is shaping society, and how society, specifically Internet users, are constructing knowledge. The design and structure of the websites presented in this article are accessed and used by Internet users who are arguably shaping how the Internet is used and perhaps the Internet itself. This phenomenon suggests that we should acknowledge the potential democratization of knowledge through the take-up of user-generated Internet sites. These websites showcase how knowledge has been obtained through experience and is being shared via the Internet medium. The article fills a gap in the literature surrounding the informal education freely available and being used globally, resulting from the online dispersion of tacit knowledge.

2. Theoretical framework

Bourdieu's (1991) key concepts of *field, capital, structuring structures and structured structures* (also known as *symbolic instruments*) provide a useful framework to analyze the structure of the websites. Bourdieu (1991) explains structuring structures to be symbolic instruments for knowing and constructing the objective world and/or symbolic forms, compared to structured structures, which he defines as means of communication, language or culture versus discourse or behavior, or symbolic objects. He claimed,

> "[t]hese classificatory schemes (structuring structures) are, essentially, the product of the incorporation of the structures of the fundamental distributions which organize the social order (structured structures)" (Bourdieu, 2000, p. 98).

Bourdieu (1992) defined a *field* as a "configuration of relations between positions objectively defined, in their existence and in the determinations they impose upon the occupants, agents or institutions" (pp. 72-73). A field represents sites of cultural practice (Webb, Schirato, & Danaher, 2002). Actions and ways of being can be generated, created and invented in each field or social space, though they are limited within the structuring mechanisms evident.

Bourdieu's forms of capital have been detailed elsewhere (e.g. Bourdieu, 1986), but it is important to clarify the states of cultural capital, that is, the *embodied* state of cultural capital includes dispositions, demeanors and character that contributes much to one's habitus. The *objectified* state of cultural capital includes the material objects and cultural goods one owns, including the quality of clothing. Finally, the *institutionalized* state of cultural capital encompasses educational qualifications in the form of legitimized certificates, diplomas and degrees.

3.   Methodology

There were 511 posts recorded via screen capture (Camtasia) and through copying and pasting textual data into Microsoft Word. The online archival research collected data over a period of four months via a daily collection of postings made within forums as well as from archived posts, and could be entitled as a "crossover" or "reengineered" methodology (Leander & McKim, 2003). The project was ethnographic-influenced in that the research aimed to capture what was going on in the familiar, naturalistic setting (that is, the particular forum they were using) of the Internet users. Instead of the researcher being a participant observer, the researcher was an observer who observed the online from the offline. This covert observation and collection of archived textual data was employed in a bid to generate understandings of the cultural practices existing online. The asynchronous research resulted with in-depth descriptions of the websites and their ways of operating, aligned with an *in situ* approach. While ethnographic principles of naturalism, discovery and understanding (Genzuk, 1999) were employed, and observation and collection of textual artifacts were the main data collection methods, the research cannot be called ethnographic (for further discussion, see Johnson & Humphry, 2012).

The project originally intended to map the online construction of knowledge through capturing, documenting and thematically analyzing the text from 12 websites and their associated discussion forums. Despite the original intent of providing data in the form of textual posts from the websites, in a bid to provide anonymity and confidentiality, it became clear that the original purpose of the research could not be achieved (for further discussion about ethical tensions, see Henderson, Johnson, & Auld, 2013). Therefore, the focus of this chapter is to explain how five of these particular websites were structured in order to showcase how knowledge and expertise are being structured and are continuing to be structured.

The data collection focused on the textual collection of comments posted in the public domain of websites that are accessible to any person browsing the Internet. Photographs or icons of users in their profiles were not captured as legal identity cannot be confirmed, nor can photographs be authentically linked to this legal identity. The prime focus was on the capturing and subsequent content analysis of the text and imagery placed within the websites of interest. This research was not focused on accurate identification of online users; instead, its focus was to explore the language used online, rather than to identify how old the users were, or their gender, or their ethnicity or cultural background. Data (textual posts) are not included in this article due to ethical concerns detailed below.

4.   Ethical considerations

Ethical permission was obtained from the university's Human Research Ethics Committee to conduct this covert form of online research. The main data reported in this article are the structure of how the websites share and construct knowledge and the ways that the notion of 'expert' is constructed and purported. While the website uniform resource locators (urls) are actual, no verbatim quotations from postings are shared due to the fact that search engines enable these textual excerpts to be traced and subsequent users identified. In addition, none of these Internet users were able to give their informed consent. That said, in considering these ethical issues, it is possible to assert the probability that no online research can ever be fully confidential, as traceability has increased and the depth of search engine potential continues to increase. One's digital footprint is difficult to erase even if a concerted effort is made to withdraw one's contributions from cyberspace (Henderson et al., 2013). Further, in an attempt to conduct online ethnographic influenced research, the ethical tension of 'lurking' became an issue (for a further discussion about 'lurking', see Johnson & Humphry, 2012). An attempt was made to peruse technical sites that were mostly frequented by adults, but as it is almost impossible to accurately define the identity of the users, it was also impossible to identify the age and ethnicity or cultural background of the users.

5. Websites that construct and shape knowledge and expertise

The following websites were located and identified as being useful to help answer the research question, and are now described as facilitating the creation of new knowledge or enabling the sharing of established knowledge. While 12 sites were selected and monitored, only the following 5 are reported on because they are the most relevant to addressing the purposes of this chapter. To delimit the scope of the study, the research assistant focused on identifying and collecting data from websites that focused on technology. As the data were collected, it became evident that the websites also structured how experts were identified and how their expertise was shared. Some of these lay experts or "experience-based experts" (Collins & Evans, 2002) are certified specialists but many are uncertified specialists, whose interactions constitute an engagement with or a contribution to a particular scientific field (Collins & Evans, 2002, 2007). Many of those positioned as experts in these forums are attributed with expertise via a social process, that is, the "socialization into the practices of an expert group" (Collins & Evans, 2007, p. 3). It should be acknowledged that the interfaces on the websites are regularly updated so what is identified and described below is not static. Generalizing the results to a broad sample of the population was not intended; the provision of the following findings and subsequent theorizing provides insight and illumination.

5.1. justanswer.com

justanswer.com is a 'professional' site where questions can be asked on any topic, and when satisfied with an answer, the 'professionals' are paid. The promotion on the home page consists of three logos that say, "Ask an Expert", "Get a Professional Answer" and "100 percent Satisfaction Guarantee (pay nothing to your expert if you're not satisfied)". The home page also showcases a range of tabs that have categories with sub-categories below each one. For instance, under the "Computers & Education" tab, the sub-categories include "Tech Support Specialists", "Networking", "Mac", "Programming", "Laptop", "Computer Hardware", "Software", etc. There is a pricing scheme for getting answers. The "experts" who answer the question receive payment for answering. Stage 1 (new) Experts earn 25 percent of what a customer is offering for an answer and Stage 4 Experts earn up to 50 percent. The person asking the question sets the price. The minimum price option is generally $9, but some categories are higher. Users can choose the higher prices based on urgency and complexity of the question. The average question costs $15. The credentials of the experts are verified by a Fortune 500 firm. Experts apply through filling out an online application, taking a short subject matter test and having their credentials such as a license, certification, two or more years of research-related employment or a Bachelor or higher degree. Once questions are 'accepted', the expert gets paid and some advertise the amount of accepted answers on their profile. Experts also display the percentage of positive feedback they have received. That said, the website includes a disclaimer about the labeling of expert: "Verification; No Reliance on the Term Expert".

Every Expert on the Site has had at least one credential relevant to the category in which they are answering questions verified by a third-party verification service. Other information about an Expert, not shown as verified, has been provided by the Expert but has not been verified. Use of the term "Expert" by JustAnswer and on the Site is only meant to describe Users who answer questions on the Site, and not to guarantee any particular level of expertise of these Experts.

Sometimes, the "expert" will have to provide extensive "customer support" service in the form of multiple queries and assistance before the "customer" will accept that they are satisfied with the answer and that the problem is fixed.

5.2.   allexperts.com

allexperts.com is a straight question and answer site. It advertises itself as "the oldest and largest free Q&A service on the Internet". It has many categories and covers most topics such as money, movies, music/performing arts, parenting/ family, real estate, recreation/outdoors, science and shopping. The "experts" are volunteers. No money, points or rewards are exchanged. Each volunteer provides a short biography giving their credentials, be it formal qualifications or interest and experience. The site claims:

> "Our experts are all volunteers, people with knowledge in their area of expertise who are willing to share their knowledge with others. We can't guarantee they can answer every question, but we can guarantee that most try to help. The really great thing about our service is that its people based – volunteers helping people without money exchanging hands!" (allexperts.com).

One of the tabs on the home page highlights the experts of the year and allocates awards for top performances, including "volunteer of the month" and "shortest average response time". The guidelines for expert volunteers state:

- You must be able to type grammatically correct English.

- You must have an above-average knowledge of the subject, although you certainly don't need to know the answers to all questions.

- You must be polite to all questioners.

- You must respond to all questions within 2-3 days, except when you go on vacation.

- You can take yourself offline during that time.

5.3. itknowledgeexchange.techtarget.com/itanswers

This website is an information technology-based knowledge sharing website. You need to be registered to ask or answer questions. They do have a points system for both the asking and answering of questions. The logo on the home page states, "Get answers. Share knowledge. Collaborate with peers".

The site advertises how to earn knowledge points that demonstrates a collaborative mentality and a means for individuals to earn social capital:

"You can easily earn Knowledge Points by contributing to the community. Here is a breakdown of how many points you can earn depending on what you do:

- Ask a Question: 5 Knowledge Points
- Answering a Question: 15 Knowledge Points
- Discussing a Question: 10 Knowledge Points
- Accepting an Answer: 10 Knowledge Points – approve an answer a fellow member has give[n] to your question

We will be highlighting the top ten contributors to the community throughout the site so start earning your Knowledge Points today. To view the point total of any user, simply click on their handle to view their profile" (itknowledgeexchange.techtarget.com/itanswers).

The users are also able to earn "badges". There was no indication of how these were earned/gained. At the time of the research, the top contributor had 59,930 points and the following badges: platinum, gold, silver, bronze, moderator, blogger, featured member and contest winner. When viewing his profile on the website, one can see his name, occupation, place of residence, a short biography, his blog or personal website, and his area(s) of expertise. The profile page also highlights his experience by topic, stating whether he is a "brainiac", "genius" or "nerd".

The site is specifically for questions about information technology (IT). There is a section where many blogs are featured, but there is no 'lounge' or general discussion area. In fact in the instructions for posting a question, it states that "job postings, homework assignments and advertising-based messages will be deleted". It is an active site with many questions being added per day.

Each question has an answer wiki, where answers can be improved. The history of answers and their revisions can also be viewed. There is also a place where the answers can be discussed and notifications of new postings can be made by Really Simple Syndication (RSS) feeds.

5.4.   tech-faq.com

The home page of this site states:

> "Tech-FAQ is a comprehensive resource of information about technology. It is built by people who believe in technology and its transformative powers to help you efficiently use technology to achieve your goals, and as a result improve your life. We have created over four thousand pages of unique and compelling content about the ever progressing technology that makes our world great. We hope that you enjoy them and that they make a positive impact on your life" (tech-faq.com).

They had 6,136 members as on 17 February 2011. When members ask questions, they receive replies which they can/cannot accept. The responder then gets "points". There are guidelines for posting. Posting comments and being helpful earn you points of recognition that you can see on the right sidebar, if you are a registered member. This site has restructured recently (since August 2010) and non-registered users no longer can see the members and their information. Prior to August, there was public access to users' profiles and all their posts.

The site is now divided into various areas: forums, news, blogs, glossary, proxy and websites. The forums seem to be the main area of use. It is divided into three main areas: "Tech Talk", where users can post questions of a technical nature and get responses, and the "Top Bits Zone", where new members introduce themselves, post announcements and call for feedback and suggestions. The final area is the "Off Topic" area where members can use "General Chat".

5.5.   geek.com

This site allowed for feedback to questions from anyone. The site seemed to appeal to technically minded people with many of the questions and discussion focusing around technical issues to do with computers, phones, iPods, software and games. There is also a "lounge" that has general discussion areas, e.g. how to track a GPS device, what degree should I get to be in the IT field and so on.

The site works by a member opening a thread and others responding. There appears to be no criteria for "expert" status, no qualification or experience needed, merely a response to questions and the person then taking notice of the response. Examples of forums are "Gadgets", "Games" and "Tech Support", and there is a table that lists the number of topics and posts in each forum.

The people who post comments do need to be registered and this also enables a brief profile to be created. Within the profile is a list of the latest forum posts that the person has written or responded to. Other parts of the website focus on the journalistic items that promote the latest news or gadgets. There are many advertisements for new products as well as reviews and recommendations of items. There are buyer's guides as well as RSS feeds on particular topics of interest such as "Mobile" and "Apple". A "Shop" section for products is also promoted.

We can apply the concept of structuring structures and structured structures (Bourdieu, 1991) or symbolic instruments to the websites and their users. The structuring structures are these particular websites and how they are set up to convey and share knowledge (and experiences). The structured structures are the accepted ways of operating (doxic practice) within the website's forums. The discourses that are utilized and espoused demonstrate that the 'experts' are being assigned social capital, even though it may not be (or is unlikely to be) in the form of institutionalized cultural capital (certificates, degrees, diplomas).

6.   The Internet and field theory

Scollon and Scollon's (2004) nexus analysis (e.g. the moment under analysis and historical analysis of everything intersecting at that moment) closely relates to the three distinct levels of data analysis that Bourdieu advocated. Bourdieu and Wacquant (1992) synthesized Bourdieu's account of field analysis. They claimed that a researcher should be directed to consider three distinct levels, namely:

1. analyze the position of the field vis-à-vis the field of power;

2. map out the objective structure of relations between the positions occupied by agents who compete for the legitimate forms of specific authority of which the field is the site; and

3. analyse the habitus of agents; the systems of dispositions they have acquired by internalizing a determinate type of social and economic condition (Bourdieu, in Bourdieu & Wacquant, 1992, pp. 104-107; see also Mills & Gale, 2007).

In considering this framework or guideline of data analysis, the identification of the field before analyzing the position of the field is necessary. I purport that the Internet is a field (a social space) that is made up of countless sub-fields. While it can also be called an environment that is made up of networks, it is useful to think of each field and the negotiations within as being representative of both virtual and biological lives, or in real life. For instance, if I am an IT consultant who is able to share my expertise and knowledge with others online, while also doing this same kind of work in my real life, then I am part of that field of interest in both places. The online forum is itself a sub-field which can transcend time and space virtually and biologically.

To give another example, if I am a teacher in my real life and yet am interested in family history and negotiate online genealogy forums making irregular posts in my spare time, I am only participating in the online sub-field of genealogy. I am not participating in the real life sub-field of genealogy though it is a possibility. The habitus that is part of the field may only constitute the digital aspects of my life; in fact it may be a segregated digital habitus, only evident when I engage in the online sub-field of which I am particularly interested.

As can be seen from the description of the websites showcased above, each of the online communities evident in the forums are specific areas of interest; there are sub-sub-fields within each forum. These online communities set up those who are esteemed, that is, those who have the symbolic capital (Bourdieu, 1986) and accepted practice within the field (Bourdieu, 2000) to be positioned as experts. These ongoing structuring structures help to perpetuate the symbolic capital exhibited by these lay experts. The structured structures that constructed the current position of these lay experts are negotiable, non-traditional and non-linear pathways (as suggested by my previous works, see Johnson, 2009a, 2009b, 2009c).

How might the position of this field be analyzed in regard to other fields? Regardless of whether readers agree that the Internet overall is a field, what we must do is compare website forums like these (sub-fields) with the field of power. Previously, authoritative knowledge could be found within textbooks or encyclopedias, written by those with high levels of institutionalized forms of capital and perhaps of economic capital. Web 1.0 opened the door for those with computer programming language knowledge to generate content, arguably another elitist form of sharing information. Social media has enabled almost anybody of any age with access to the Internet to position them in an authoritative or expert-like way. This is not without its problems or complexities, but it does mean that the Internet by its very user-generated nature can be egalitarian, enabling users to distribute their voice more easily, and society can be less reliant on hierarchical authority associated with institutional capital.

The Internet is also a field of research that has been opened up to researchers to explore. This can be done via the type of research conducted (online surveys for instance), but also as sub-fields that are representative of sub-fields within real life. Discussions surrounding the validity of online research and authenticity of users have been discussed elsewhere (e.g. Johnson, 2011; Lefever, Dal, & Matthíasdóttir, 2006; Williams, 2007) but this also demonstrates how the Internet is its own independent field, but yet can also be closely linked with fields or sub-fields that existed before the Internet or are in current coexistence between virtual and analogue lives.

In this chapter, I map out the relational structure of multiple agents who are competing for legitimization of their knowledge. However, there are severe limitations in being able to fully analyze the habitus of the agents. If Internet users are identifiable, we cannot be sure of their authentic identities; therefore, we can only conjecture the acquired system of dispositions. Only the captured prose from the forums could be used to explore this third level (as suggested by Bourdieu & Wacquant, 1992), but as stated earlier, it is unethical to present this prose because of the possible identification of Internet users.

6.1.   Structured structures

Pre-Internet, knowledge and expertise were established by institutional structures and authoritative texts. These five websites have been constructed by non-traditional or non-institutional structures not usually associated with education or formal knowledge. Some are set up as enterprises, as commercial entities whereby knowledge is a commodity. However, they also shape the Internet by enabling the continuity of autonomy, independence and flexibility. These symbolic instruments contribute to the continued construction of knowledge and expertise. This is being done without the validation of external verifications, qualifications and attestations (though on some websites, listing these is a requirement). It is being done through peer validation and affirmation; yet, there are repercussions. If you do not know your stuff, you do not get paid (or validated) on justanswer.com. On the other websites, if you do not offer answers or advice that is accepted then your social capital will not be validated.

6.2. Privileged and marginalized knowledges

Harwood (2004) terms privileged knowledges as "dominant knowledges", typically those that are knowledges which are school-centric, or institution-centric. Those that value dominant knowledges do not value non-institutionalized productions of knowledge. The dominant knowledges we as academics praise are ones that meet hierarchical and developmental forms of achievement surrounding the progressive (linear) mastery of content. We value those that have objectified cultural capital (Bourdieu, 1986) in the form of certificates or degrees. This has been brought about by being positioned "in scholastic universes resulting from a long process of autonomization" (Bourdieu, 2000, p. 25). It seems the user-generated version of the Internet is a social condition that enables the generation of cultural products or contemporary knowledge, self-evident through the active production, consumption and fluid modification of user-generated websites.

Supposed authoritative texts such as books can be disregarded in favor of seeking "practical wisdom" (Beckett, 1995) from Internet users seeking answers to questions from real people. These 'sites' could be considered to be symbolic instruments where marginalized knowledges are represented. By some, they might be considered erudite knowledges, but by most, their constructions and outworkings are marginalized. Just like gamers whose skills are considered irrelevant depending on the field in which they are positioned, their knowledge is valued. Despite that, many of the experts promulgated within these websites do not possess institutionalized cultural capital in the form of formal educational qualifications.

These experts are perceived to possess knowledge that firstly has been validated by other users (or the structures of the website); therefore, they have been approved to share it, or these experts are in the process of becoming validated by other users and thus are involved in a process of earning embodied cultural capital. They are self-nominated as experts or as being able to provide useful answers, sharing knowledge from their own experience. This kind of knowledge is different to traditional constructions of institutionalized or privileged knowledge.

6.3.   The 'no zone' of action

Digitization and flexibility means there are 'no zones' of when things 'can' or 'are allowed to be' done. Language can be far more direct, blunt, reckless, yet, far less reliant on policy, bureaucracy, restraints or having to 'do' what is expected. There is far more freedom available online than in real life, partly because of the possible degree of anonymity able to be gained through posting content online.

The online freedom (an aspect of democracy) means that postings can be made with limited repercussions and limited accountability. However, there is documentation of lawsuits and charges being made, or jobs being lost because of inappropriate Facebook statuses and the like. Admittedly, what does occur on the Internet are new "stakes of the game" (Bourdieu, 2000, p. 151). This means that there are not those social cues or inhibitions we may impose or others impose on ourselves. The reality is that comments are made to others online that would never be made in real life or face-to-face, even on the phone.

Derogatory put-downs or off-the-cuff statements are made without any thoughts of consequences of possible inappropriate use of a forum. Private issues become far more public and are instantly done. It does give some a sense of power and a sense of more agency because they can vent online, and in some cases, are able to attract empathy and support (even for fictional, or secretive narratives). This medium means we find out more about others and their personal lives, and private thoughts are made more public –we have insight seldom possible before the advent and take-up of social media.

Instead of only those who are in power being privileged to share and publish results via privileged forms of knowledge, those with marginalized knowledges are now able to do so. More Internet users are able to have a voice with social media; power appears to be more equally distributed. This is particularly the case with the reporting that occurs via the media. Who decides what to report, and when, and how much will be repeated or focused upon? With the Internet, there are no pathways that must be journeyed, no rituals that must be completed (or qualifications that must be gained) and no institutional regulations that must be adhered to, that is, no institutionalized cultural capital. Those with Internet access can report things from wherever they are within any forum via any digital means. To me, this means that power is no longer held within the Press and the gatekeepers. There are few gatekeepers (for the most part) that determine who can have a voice, and who can position themselves as an expert.

Users are able to claim their form of cultural capital via how they access, use and post on Internet forums. Many of them eschew what little capital they have via ranting and have no interest in deliberation or negotiation with others (Loveland & Popescu, 2011). Therefore, while the web is seemingly more egalitarian because more people can have a voice, hereby demonstrating horizontal, rather than hierarchical positioning, multi-dimensional societal factors still affect the field in which they are positioned (Tacchi, 2012). If I make a post in a field that I know a lot about and am able to state my experience, qualifications and nous within the field depending on what forum I utilize, I might be able to claim the symbolic or virtual capital in actuality. If I contribute to a forum where I have limited knowledge of that particular field, I cannot lay claim to any capital that may be actual or virtual, real or symbolic, biological in real life or contrived within cyberspace. This contrived explanation may be realistic or false.

While almost anybody can position themselves as an expert on the Internet, not all are verified and accepted as experts. Despite the possibility of being able to obtain this form of capital, few (in the scheme of things) are ratified as experts. Validation or affirmation of expertise may occur through the structures of the website which is being formally utilized, or may be informally eschewed through popularity, namely the volume of other Internet users who are fans of a particular virtual entity. Again, this relates to what is valued or powerful within a field or social space. Each of these websites has their social agents within the field of interest that the website is advocating. These social agents have constructed the power and authority of the lay knowledge evident and espoused by these users, but this is structured by the structure of the websites –the zones of accepted (doxic) practice.

7.   Conclusion

The findings of this research suggest that the nature of knowledge is now far more fluid than prior to pre-Web 2.0. The content generated by users who participate in these online forums conveys that knowledge is now mediated and shared discursively via digital actors within society. The way experts are positioned within these forums, that is, the structuring structures such as justanswer.com and allanswers.com, allows for a degree of consensus as to the validation of lay experts, and also those who do have formal qualifications. The distributed nature of access challenges a hierarchical sense of authority, though admittedly brings with it a multiplicity of further issues (Tacchi, 2012). A democratic consensus validates the lay experts' 'know-how'. Digital participants utilize the structured structures to comment on whether statements are accurate or contestable, and the increasing accessibility to the Internet for many people (not all people) means that far more people are enabled to have a voice. They can have power not available to them in their real lives, because of the relative anonymity and egalitarian nature of the Internet environment. The symbolic instruments captured at this time in this site of engagement demonstrate that many Internet users' agency is performed as these structuring structures and structured structures enable them to act on the virtual world in a way not possible to many of them in their real lives.

References

Beckett, D. (1995). Professional practice for educators: The getting of wisdom? *Educational Philosophy and Theory, 27*(2), 15-34. doi:10.1111/j.1469-5812.1995.tb00237.x

Bourdieu, P. (1986). The forms of capital. In J. E. Richardson (Ed.), *Handbook of theory of research for the sociology of education* (pp. 241-258). Westport, CT: Greenword Press.

Bourdieu, P. (1990/1980). *The logic of practice* [Translated by Richard Nice]. Stanford, CA: Stanford University Press.

Bourdieu, P. (1991). *Language and symbolic power*. Cambridge: Polity Press.

Bourdieu, P. (1992). *The rules of art*. Cambridge: Polity Press.

Bourdieu, P. (2000). *Pascalian meditations*. Cambridge: Polity Press.

Bourdieu, P., & Wacquant, L. J. D. (1992). *An invitation to reflexive sociology*. Chicago, IL: University of Chicago Press.

Collins, H. M., & Evans, R. (2002). The third wave of science studies: Studies of expertise and experience. *Social Studies of Science, 32*(2), 235-296. doi:10.1177/0306312702032002003

Collins, H. M., & Evans, R. (2007). *Rethinking expertise*. Chicago, IL: University of Chicago Press. doi:10.7208/chicago/9780226113623.001.0001

Genzuk, M. (1999). Tapping into community funds of knowledge. In *Effective strategies for English language acquisition: A curriculum guide for the development of teachers, grades Kindergarten through eight*. Los Angeles: Los Angeles Annenberg Metropolitan Project/ ARCO Foundation. Retrieved from http://www-bcf.usc.edu/~genzuk/Genzuk_ARCO_ Funds_of_Knowledge.pdf

Harwood, V. (2004). Subject to scrutiny: Taking Foucauldian genealogies to narratives of youth oppression. In M. L. Rasmussen, E. Rofes, & S. Talburt (Eds), *Youth and sexualities: Pleasure, subversion, and insubordination in and out of schools* (pp. 85-108). New York: Palgrave Macmillan.

Henderson, M., Johnson, N. F., & Auld, G. (2013). Silences of ethical practice: Dilemmas for researchers using social media. *Educational Research and Evaluation, 19*(6), 546-560. doi:10.1080/13803611.2013.805656

Johnson, N. F. (2009a). The teenage expertise network: The online availability of expertise. *International Journal of Learning, 16*(5), 211-220.

Johnson, N. F. (2009b). Teenage technological experts' views of schooling. *Australian Educational Researcher, 36*(1), 59-72. doi:10.1007/BF03216892

Johnson, N. F. (2009c). Cyber-relations in the field of home computer use for leisure: Bourdieu and teenage technological experts. *E-Learning, 6*(2), 187-197. doi:10.2304/ elea.2009.6.2.187

Johnson, N. F. (2011). No, they're not digital natives and they're not addicted: An essay critiquing contestable labels. *Fast Capitalism, 8*(2). Retrieved from http://www.fastcapitalism.com

Johnson, N. F., & Humphry, N. (2012). The teenage expertise network (TEN): An online ethnographic approach. *International Journal of Qualitative Studies in Education, 25*(6), 723-739. doi:10.1080/09518398.2011.590160

Kahne, J., Middaugh, E., Lee, N.-J., & Feezell, J. T. (2012). Youth online activity and exposure to diverse perspectives. *New Media & Society, 14*(3), 492-512. doi:10.1177/1461444811420271

Leander, K. M., & McKim, K. K. (2003). Tracing the everyday "Sitings" of adolescents on the Internet: A strategic adaptation of ethnography across online and offline spaces. *Education, Communication and Information, 3*(2), 211-240. doi:10.1080/14636310303140

Lefever, S., Dal, M., & Matthíasdóttir, Á. (2006). Online data collection in academic research: Advantages and limitations. *British Journal of Educational Technology, 38*(4), 574-582. doi:10.1111/j.1467-8535.2006.00638.x

Loveland, M. T., & Popescu, D. (2011). Democracy on the web: Assessing the deliberative qualities of Internet forums. *Information, Communication & Society, 14*(5), 684-703. doi:10.1080/1369118X.2010.521844

Mills, C., & Gale, T. (2007). Researching social inequalities in education: Towards a Bourdieuian methodology. *International Journal of Qualitative Studies in Education, 20*(4), 433-447. doi:10.1080/09518390601176523

Scollon, R., & Scollon, S. W. (2004). *Nexus analysis: Discourse and the emerging Internet.* New York: Routledge.

Tacchi, J. (2012). Open content creation: The issues of voice and the challenges of listening. New Media & Society, 14(4), 652-668. doi:10.1177/1461444811422431

Webb, J., Schirato, T., & Danaher, G. (2002). Understanding Bourdieu. Crows Nest: Allen and Unwin.

Vromen, A. (2011). Constructing Australian youth online. *Information, Communication & Society, 14*(7), 959-980. doi:10.1080/1369118X.2010.549236

Williams, M. (2007). Avatar watching: Participant observation in graphical online environments. *Qualitative Research, 7*(1), 5-24. doi:10.1177/1468794107071408

8 The Internet: Friend, foe or target?

Jonathan D. James[1]

The eye never has enough of seeing (Ecclesiastes 1:8).

Wisdom is supreme, therefore get wisdom. Though it cost all you have,
get understanding... embrace her, and she will honor you (Proverbs 4:7-8).

Keywords: Internet perils and prospects, Internet future, post privacy, surveillance, China and Internet.

1.   Introduction

While talking to a friend a few months ago, I heard a rather distressing story. Andrew, my friend who had just lost his 95-year old father, said this of his dad: "Apparently he was not significant in this life… because I did an Internet search on him and nothing showed up". Is our worth today measured in the number of search hits that appear about us on the Internet? In this respect, Michael Jaffarian's question in relation to the Internet, in chapter 4, "what will this do to us?", is rather insightful and penetrating.

In this concluding chapter, I give an overview of how the Internet, a byproduct of our times, is shaping our culture and society in profound ways. I note some of the major concerns and perils of the Internet age and I conclude by pointing out how and why certain countries are targeting the Internet in terms of increased regulation and surveillance.

1. E-mail address: aefi@iinet.net.au

How to cite this chapter: James, J. D. (2014). The Internet: Friend, foe or target?. In J. D. James (Ed.), *The Internet and the Google age: Prospects and perils* (pp. 153-169). Dublin: Research-publishing.net. doi:10.14705/rpnet.2014.000183

2.   A culture of technology

Each new medium brings with it a revolution which results in major changes in culture and in the organization of society (DeFleur & Ball-Rokeach, 1982). The culture of our times influences the media of tomorrow. No medium exists in a vacuum. The need for instant communication, instant results and fast food reveals a culture that wants to get the most out of life in the quickest possible time frame using the fastest means available. Add this phenomenon to the technological inventions of the preceding generation (such as the newspaper, radio, television, etc.), and this provides the seed bed for the invention of a new medium relevant for the times (DeFleur & Ball-Rokeach, 1982). The Internet, like every communication medium, is both a cause and effect of the times we live in. It was caused by the complex circumstances of modern times and, as an effect, it is impacting post-modern lives.

It is no coincidence that the Internet was developed initially as a military communications system[1]. This accounts for its logical operating system based on digital technology, its relative speed and the initial cloak of secrecy:

> "The Internet was first invented for military purposes, and then expanded to the purpose of communication among scientists. The invention also came about in part by the increasing need for computers in the 1960s. During the Cold War, it was essential to have communications links between military and university computers that would not be disrupted by bombs or enemy spies. In order to solve the problem, in 1968 DARPA (Defense Advanced Research Projects Agency) made contracts with BBN (Bolt, Beranek and Newman) to create ARPANET (Advanced Research Projects Agency Network)" (Gharbawi, 1991, para. 3).

So from secretive communication within the military to guarded scientific inquiry, the Internet has become an everyday tool for the common person, to

---

[1]. In the introductory chapter it was mentioned that electronic warfare would be the next phase of the Internet. If this happens, then the Internet would have come full circle –starting as a military communication tool and advancing to become a weapon to shut down the electronic technology of the enemy.

be used in homes, offices, businesses and factories as "the largest network of networks worldwide" (Gharbawi, 1991, para. 2). Internet technology has filtered down into the hands of the masses. Hence, the Internet age is a culture of technology, easily accessed and navigated by close to 3 billion people[1] (Internet World Stats website, 2014). Imagine how life would be without this medium of communication. Indeed, life and society today are organized around the Internet, and young children are acculturated into the culture of technology even before they learn the alphabet and are admitted into school.

The emergence of new gadgets, be it Smartphones, tablets, iPads or the like, has introduced a new way of life and indeed a new perception of life, but the impact of these on society remains to be fully grasped.

Internet technology is changing ever so rapidly (this could be another characteristic of the Internet age) and it seems that users are going along with the changes, but these changes have implications:

> "Unlike many previous technologies like the television or telephone, social media applications evolve far more quickly, often without warning and in ways that may have significant implications for users and their practices. Social media researchers may be halfway through data collection when they discover that an important feature has been redesigned or removed altogether" (Ellison & Boyd, 2013, p. 164).

3.   Major concerns

The virtues and potentials of the Internet are well known, and the foregoing chapters have clearly illustrated them. Groundbreaking studies on social network sites such as Facebook and Twitter have been undertaken (Park & Kastanis, 2009), and the educational benefits of the Internet are becoming more and more

---

1. The world's population is approximately 7.2 billion people as of June, 2014, (Worldometers website, n.d.) so the Internet is still not accessible to large segments of the world. Technology must be aided by public policy to ensure that Internet education, facilities and access are equally available to all sectors of the community to prevent the phenomenon of 'digital divide' referred to in chapter 1 by Iremae D. Labucay.

apparent. Recently, Souleles (2012), used action research to study the effects of embedding Facebook in an undergraduate communications course where students identified several educational benefits, including useful feedback from both peers and teachers.

However, as foreshadowed in the introductory chapter, the Internet and all its multi-faceted platforms have brought a cluster of moral and ethical concerns. A selected list is briefly discussed below in the hope that it will serve as a catalyst for more sustained research in the near future.

3.1.　An era of post-privacy?

Teitelbaum (1996), in *Wired* magazine, made an astonishing statement about the realities of life in the Internet age: "Privacy is history –get over it".

Yet, according to a host of civil and political organizations,

> "[p]rivacy is a fundamental human right recognized in the UN Declaration of Human Rights, the International Covenant on Civil and Political Rights and in many other international and regional treaties. Privacy underpins human dignity and other key values such as freedom of association and freedom of speech. It has become one of the most important human rights issues of the modern age" (GILC website, n.d.).

The paradox is that, unlike any other period in human history, today people are willingly revealing their most intimate and personal details via the Internet. The extraordinary growth of social networking sites, such as Facebook and Twitter, have opened the door for people to reveal personal details in the public sphere. People are encouraged, and even given the 'start up' tools by social networking sites, to intentionally create profiles to communicate with and develop existing friendships, grow new relationships, and locate friends from the past. Sadly, some users naively treat sites such as Facebook as a private web paradise. As noted by Papacharissi (2011), "[t]echnology may provide the stage for this interaction, linking the individual, separately or simultaneously, with multiple audiences. Online social networks constitute such sites of self presentation and identity negotiation" (p. 304).

Thus the projection of one's self, and the need to "keep up with the Joneses", overrides all other concerns, including privacy concerns, and as Tamir and Mitchell (2012) discovered, 80 percent of all blogs and posts in social media sites are in essence texts and images related to personal details, experiences and announcements. In short, self-disclosure constitutes the main content on social media. Apparently, the more you share the more you gain. However, with this 'sharing' comes a litany of potential dangers, such as privacy invasion, loss of confidentiality, damage to reputation, and even identity theft.

Nissenbaum (2010) has revealed that search engine companies routinely keep a log of all searches for a period of time and that various governments, including the USA, have been known to subpoena these companies during critical times for records of certain users and searches.

Tavani (2012) goes a step further to argue that individual searches made by users can easily be converted into profiles that could be potentially sold to commercial companies, thus revealing the dark side of what could happen in our merged technological and capitalistic society. Recently, it was revealed that Facebook has a fairly large group of in-house researchers who routinely dig into Facebook's database of approximately 1.3 billion users to study trends in user content and other related matters (Albergotti, 2014). Anecdotal evidence suggests that it is commonplace for employers and recruiters to use Facebook and other social media platforms to make assessments of current and would-be employees.

Vaidhyanathan (2011) warns of the hidden dangers of "Googlization":

> "we are not Google's customers: we are its product. We –our fancies, fetishes, predilections, and preferences– are what Google sells to advertisers. When we use Google to find out things on the Web, Google uses our Web searches to find out things about us" (p. 3).

A related issue as pointed out by Nicola Johnson in chapter 7 is this: is our Internet footprint permanent? Hence we can expect that privacy concerns and the protection of our personal information, together with litigation cases, will become more and more prominent in the digital age. Critical studies on the Internet seek to address these issues:

> "a critical contribution to Internet privacy studies makes an effort to the individual role of control and choice as well as to the constraining effects of social structures on Web 2.0 platforms and social networking sites such as Facebook, Twitter, Myspace, YouTube, and Blogger. It furthermore investigates the principle of Web 2.0 platforms, that is the massive provision and storage of personal identifiable data that are systematically evaluated, marketed, and used for targeted advertising [...]. A critical notion of Internet privacy wants to put privacy threats and ownership structures of such commercial platforms into the larger context of societal problems in public discourse" (Allmer, 2013, section 5).

Therefore, it is important for users to be aware of the ethical and legal implications of self-disclosure and for Internet agencies and social media sites to have clear and transparent policies in place.

3.2.   'Anti social' media?

Picture a typical family of four in the USA or any first-world nation having dinner at a restaurant. Each one is engaged with his or her own Smartphone and iPad answering emails, involved in games, listening to music, or messaging and exchanging photographs. In this scenario, the family members are indeed 'connecting', but not with one another as members of a family.

The function of social media is to connect people, and users of Facebook and other platforms are known to have many 'friends'. However quantity seems to override quality in these relationships and closeness does not seem to be achieved, because each user constantly looks for "one more friend" to add.

Because an average Facebook user has 300-500 friends, this begs the question: are they real friends?

FriendFolio is a new and daring game purporting to find out how much our friends on social sites are worth and how that value can be added to the user:

> "If you have quite a few friends on Facebook, FriendFolio [...] wants to be your guide as to how much they're worth. Launched by London-based application builder BAPPZ, FriendFolio does on the Web precisely what investors in the real world cannot do, which is: buy, sell, and trade friends. (At least not overtly, anyway.) That's right, no more equality for all [...]. The developers behind FriendFolio consider it Facebook users' right to place one another on a marketplace gauged in dollars and cents and strategize their way to higher-than-thou status.
>
> Want to get rich? You sure can. By playing your ambition card(s) especially well with those carefully honed skills derived from countless hours passing go on [sic] within that capitalistic wonderworld called Monopoly –plus a good amount of 'friendly' exploitation– you can build quite an impressive portfolio of Facebook associates through FriendFolio that the application's developers would like to describe as nothing less than a game for beautiful people, CEOs, and Apprentice hopefuls" (Glazowski, 2008, para. 2-3).

3.3. 'Selfies' and narcissism

A new word has been coined for a phenomenon that has come into being on the Internet –the growing number of 'selfies'. A 'selfie' "is a picture of yourself [taken by you] usually shared on any social networking website" (Moreau, n.d., para. 2). Moreau (n.d.) also goes on to suggest several reasons why this trend of posting self-taken photos is growing;

- to get attention from as many people as possible;
- to get a self-esteem boost;

- to show off;
- to get a specific person's attention;
- boredom;
- because social media is fun.

Are social media sites pandering to the narcissistic nature of post-modern people where 'self' has become the new focus? Twitter is a micro blogging site where people share frequently about such things as where they have been, what they have eaten, what books they have read and what they have achieved. Thus, the 'followers', who read a particular tweet, get to hear about all the trivial and mundane details of a person's activities.

The university of Salford in the UK did a study on social media's effects on a person's self-esteem with the following results:

"50% of their 298 participants said that their use of social networks like Facebook and Twitter makes their lives worse [...]. In addition to this, a quarter of participants cited work or relationship difficulties because of 'online confrontations', and more than half reported that they feel 'worried or uncomfortable' when they can't access Facebook or email. In sum, this study concluded that social media causes low self-esteem and anxiety" (Soltero, n.d., para. 2).

If our sense of identity and worth is constantly impacted and measured by what other people are doing as they continuously post images, updates, events and tweets on social sites, then people could be setting themselves up for failure and emotional distress.

3.4. Ambiguity

Anyone today can start up a website, post a blog, or become a member of an interactive community. Even terrorist organizations use social media platforms and have their own websites. This sense of democracy and egalitarianism is to be celebrated, but the downside is that there may be a sense of ambiguity for the everyday user who is confused by the multiplicity and sometimes conflicting accounts of views or information on any given issue. Therefore, the 'wisdom of the masses' in this instance may be inconsequential or even harmful. This in no way contradicts Levy's (1997) findings that the Internet introduces "the construction of intelligent communities in which social and cognitive potential can be mutually developed" (p. 17). It merely shows that the cacophony of voices in cyberspace is a reality and users need wisdom and insight to make correct judgments.

Köerner (n.d.) gives a personalized account of how the Internet can entice a person to search and browse from one website to another –creating almost a form of addiction, or 'electronic narcotics':

> "Spend thirty minutes 'surfing the web' and do your best to retain your sense of self. The more I aimlessly wander down the rabbit holes of media that prostitute themselves across my screen, the more I degenerate into a glazed-over zombie, hungry and manic yet lacking any sense of purpose. In this state of mind, it's easier to be pulled into the downward spiral than to slap myself awake, and I quickly feel full and exhausted by the wretchedness of all that I have consumed" (Köerner, n.d., para. 1).

We referred earlier in the introductory chapter to Suler's (2004) study on disinhibition; the above comments make sense when seen in the light of his psychological study.

3.5.   'Communication overload'

The preponderance of emails, text messages, blogs, Facebook notifications and the like are all adding to a condition of 'communication overload'. This phenomenon of continuous communication is illustrated in this striking set of research statistics: in 2012, an average of 144 billion emails were sent per day, together with 1 billion Facebook messages or updates and 47 billion instant text messages (Cirius website, 2012; Radicati, 2012). Think of the time an average person spends on any given day deleting unwanted, insignificant or dated emails, text messages, social media updates, invitations and the like.

Our lives are changing but, more importantly, our perception of life may also be affected in the process. Psychologist Cook (2014) highlights what she terms 'emerging adults', and explains this by giving a scenario of a 27-year-old child who plays video games on the computer in his pajamas most of the day. Therefore, growing up in this culture of technology can pose unique challenges for both parents and children:

> "Our private sphere has ceased to be the stage where drama of the subject at odds with his objects and with his image is played out: we no longer exist as playwrights or actors but as terminals of multiple networks" (Baudrillard, 1987, p. 16).

3.6. Fragmentation

As mentioned earlier, anyone and everyone can potentially launch their own website to promote their own views, hobbies, political ideas, religious beliefs, values and judgments. Hence, the Internet can become "all things to all people". In time, people with particular tastes and views may, by choice, only log onto the sites that reinforce their particular views and tastes. The Internet may follow the way of established media such as TV and radio, which have moved from traditional broadcasting to 'narrowcasting'. A narrow cast is defined as data being sent to

> "a specific list of recipients. Cable television is an example of narrowcasting since the cable TV signals are sent only to homes that have subscribed to the cable service. In contrast, network TV uses a broadcast model in which the signals are transmitted everywhere and anyone with an antenna can receive them" (Webopedia website, n.d.).

In light of the perils of the Internet, and the fact that human nature (which is responsible for many of the dark aspects of the Internet) is not likely to change, we believe that what is needed is for schools, institutions and community groups to create or weave into existing curricula a comprehensive manual for educating people in navigating and negotiating life on the Internet, with learning goals such as these to

- discover sensible ways to handle the Internet;

- acquire wisdom and guidance to be aware of the Internet's dark side (it can be argued that whereas 'information' and facts can be quickly 'googled', wisdom does not come that easily with the click of a browser);

- have access to preventive measures for Internet addiction and communication overload;

- lead a balanced life which also includes time for outdoor activities, face-to-face interaction with family and friends, etc.

Many of the resources for such goals are already available online and the research done by psychologists, such as Suler (2004), Barak and Suler (2008), Finfgeld (1999) and Cook (2014) are useful starting points.

4. Internet - the target of certain nations

Social networking sites and related platforms have been used successfully by citizens to topple governments and overturn policies in countries such as Iran, Egypt and Colombia. As a backlash, repressive regimes such as China, North Korea and Vietnam seem to be tightening their grip on Internet surveillance.

Internet usage around the world is increasing. Asia, with its teeming population, is leading the way in Internet usage and is poised for explosive growth in the coming years. China, the most populous nation in the world, has approximately 600 million Internet users, with an Internet penetration of nearly 45 percent (Reporters without Borders website, n.d.).

Even so, we recognize that an increase in Internet usage does not guarantee democratization, as some countries are wrestling with the Internet and have strong regulations in place. In the introductory chapter, we gave six characteristics of the Internet, and it seems likely that another characteristic needs to be mentioned: the Internet is built on openness and the democratic principle that everyone is able to access a free flow of information. Social media promotes this principle by giving people a voice so that opinions and views can be exchanged. It is therefore not surprising that the democratic nature of the Internet poses a threat to authoritarian regimes whose ideologies are based on the notion that absolute power should rest in the hands of those in political leadership.

China leads the way in the art of Internet surveillance with its infamous "Great Firewall of China", a term used to refer to China's massive Internet filtering and censorship system. The Chinese Communist Party has judiciously licensed eight service providers for this nation of 1.3 billion people (Reporters without Borders website, n.d.). In China, there are at least five government departments that are involved in censorship and surveillance of the Internet on a multi-layered basis (Reporters without Borders website, n.d.). In addition, there is a special Internet police force to monitor what the public is posting on the net through any Internet platforms. This is all part of a larger plan to control the Internet in this nation:

> "criminal statutes were revised to allow for the prosecution of online subversion, limiting direct foreign investment in Internet companies and requiring companies to register with the information that might harm unification of the country, endanger national security, or subvert the government. Promoting 'evil cults' (an obvious reference to Beijing's campaign against Falun Gong) was similarly banned, along with anything that 'disturbs social order'" (Press Reference website, n.d.).

The level of censorship is so extensive in China that even the Internet Search giant Google left Mainland China in 2010 and moved its China operations to Hong Kong[1] (Helft, 2010).

---

1. Hong Kong used to be a British colony until 1997 when it was returned to Chinese hands. Since the return, Hong Kong remains as a Special Administrative Region of China (SAR), and retains its capitalistic economy and a certain measure of its democratic policies.

Wong (2010), from the Center of Democracy and Technology, describes how China's Government has successfully used the Internet for its own ends, thus providing a 'model' for other authoritarian nations:

"China and other regimes have demonstrated that the internet can be introduced into the population without functioning as a liberalizing force. In fact, the Chinese government frequently employs the [I]nternet to shape political debates" (para. 5).

Harvard scholar Penney (2013) summarizes the situation in China, suggesting that even in this repressive system there may be creative ways to overcome controls and, perhaps, a window of opportunity for a change of sorts:

"The scale and penetration of internet use among Chinese citizens is extraordinary, and there are only so many internet police and web commentators you can hire to contain 'problematic' internet content. It also means that more Chinese citizens will gain the technical knowledge to find more means to circumvent filtering methods. These are definitely interesting times" (last para.).

5. Conclusion

The Internet is a friend to many people, a foe to some, and a target for a few repressive governments. Notwithstanding, the Internet, according to many experts, will flourish and become more and more interwoven into the very fabric of our lives. The Pew Research Center and Elon University study, which interviewed several experts, found that the Internet "will become like electricity during the next decade, less visible but more important and embedded in everyday life" (Shirvell, 2014, para. 5). The study also revealed that there were as many negatives as positives, because people today are becoming more aware of the perils of the Internet: "[t]hey worry about interpersonal ethics, surveillance, terror and crime and the inevitable backlash as governments and industry try to adjust" (Shirvell, 2014, para. 8).

We started this book with a reference to the Internet's 25th anniversary in 2014. The results of the European Union study, which look futuristically to the Internet's next 15 years, is a fitting way to conclude the book:

> "If the Internet could wish for anything on its 40th birthday, it would probably ask to be more powerful, connected and intuitive –responding to our needs at home, work or on the go […]. This is how the future internet is evolving: as an internet of services, things and infrastructure. From smart appliances that talk to each other to clothes that monitor our health; from cars that cannot crash to mobile technologies and cloud platforms that run our businesses" (Digital Agenda for Europe website, n.d.).

Get ready for life in an incredibly more digitalized world!

References

Albergotti, R. (2014, July 4). Facebook study poor: Sandberg. *The Australian*. Retrieved from http://www.theaustralian.com.au/business/wall-street-journal/facebook-study-poor-sandberg/story-fnay3ubk-1226976954342

Allmer, T. (2013). Critical Internet privacy studies. *Fast Capitalism*. Retrieved from http://www.uta.edu/huma/agger/fastcapitalism/10_1/allmer10_1.html

Barak, A., & Suler, J. (2008). Reflections on the psychology and social science of cyberspace. In A. Barak & J. Suler (Eds), *Psychological aspects of cyberspace: Theory, research, applications*. Cambridge, UK: Cambridge University Press. doi:10.1017/CBO9780511813740.002

Baudrillard, J. (1987). *The ecstasy of communication* [Translated by Bernard and Caroline Schutz]. Paris: Galilee.

Cook, K. V. (2014, July 14). Growing up now: A brief guide for emerging adults and their parents. *The Table*. Retrieved from http://goo.gl/B0b9Io

DeFleur, M. L., & Ball-Rokeach, S. (1982). *Theories of mass communication*. New York: Longman.

Ellison, N. B., & Boyd, D. M. (2013). Sociality through social network sites. In W. H. Dutton (Ed.), *The Oxford handbook of Internet studies* (pp. 151-172). Oxford: Oxford University Press.

Finfgeld, D. L. (1999). Psychotherapy in cyberspace. *Journal of American Psychiatric Nursing Association, 5*(4), 105-110. doi:10.1177/107839039900500401

Gharbawi, A. (1991). *Revolution of the Internet*. Retrieved from http://www.cs.ucsb. edu/~almeroth/classes/F04.176A/homework1_good_papers/Alaa-Gharbawi.html

Glazowski, P. (2008, April 8). FriendFolio: Buy and sell friends on Facebook. *Mashable*. Retrieved from http://mashable.com/2008/04/08/friendfolio/

Helft, M. (2010, March 22). Google shuts China site in dispute over censorship. *The New York Times*. Retrieved from http://www.nytimes.com/2010/03/23/technology/23google. html?_r=0

Holy Bible. (1984). *Holy Bible. The New International Version (NIV)*. Colorado Springs: International Bible Society.

Köerner, W. (n.d.). *Ambiguity in the age of the Internet* [Blog post]. Retrieved from http:// willakoerner.com/2013/02/20/ambiguity-in-the-age-of-the-internet/

Levy, P. (1997). *Collective intelligence: Mankind's emerging world in cyberspace* [Translated by Robert Bononno]. New York: Plenum Press.

Moreau, E. (n.d.). What is a selfie? *About Technology*. Retrieved from http://webtrends.about. com/od/Mobile-Web-Beginner/a/What-Is-A-Selfie.htm

Nissenbaum, H. (2010). *Privacy in context: Technology, policy, and the integrity of social life*. Palo Alto, California: Stanford University Press.

Papacharissi, Z. (2011). Conclusion: A networked self. In Z. Papacharissi (Ed.), *A networked self identity, community and culture on social network sites*. New York: Routledge.

Park, J. Y., & Kastanis, L. (2009). Reflective learning through social network sites in design education. *The International Journal of Learning, 16*(8), 11-22.

Penney, J. (Interviewee) & China Correspondent (Interviewer). (2013). The great Firewall of China. *Open Democracy*. Retrieved from http://www.opendemocracy.net/china-correspondent/great-firewall-of-china

Radicati, S. (Ed.). (2012). *Email Statistics Report, 2012-2016*. Palo Alto, CA: The Radicati Group, INC. A technology market research firm. Retrieved from http://www.radicati. com/wp/wp-content/uploads/2012/04/Email-Statistics-Report-2012-2016-Executive-Summary.pdf

Shirvell, B. (2014, March 11). 15 predictions for the future of the Internet. *PBS NewsHour*. Retrieved from http://www.pbs.org/newshour/rundown/15-predictions-future-internet/

Soltero, Á. J. (n.d.). The relationship between social media and self-worth. *Social Media 101*. Retrieved from http://thesocialu101.com/the-relationship-between-social-media-and-self-worth/#sthash.30W6kqzs.dpuf

Souleles, N. (2012). An action research project on the use of Facebook in an undergraduate visual communication study unit. *Art, Design & Communication in Higher Education, 11*(2), 127-141.

Suler, J. (2004). The online disinhibition effect. *Cyberpsychology & Behaviour, 7*(3), 321-326. doi:10.1089/1094931041291295

Tamir, D. I., & Mitchell, J. P. (2012). Disclosing information about the self is intrinsically rewarding. *Proceedings of the National Academy of Sciences, 109*(21), 8038-8043. doi:10.1073/pnas.1202129109

Tavani, H. (2012). Search engines and ethics. In E. N. Zalta (Ed.), *The Stanford encyclopedia of Philosophy*. Spring 2014. Retrieved from http://plato.stanford.edu/archives/spr2014/entries/ethics-search/

Teitelbaum, S. (1996). Privacy is history –get over it. *Wired magazine, On Newsstands Now, 4*(2). Retrieved from http://archive.wired.com/wired/archive/4.02/brin.html

Vaidhyanathan, S. (2011). *The Googlization of everything (and why we should worry)*. Berkely, CA: University of California Press.

Wong, C. (Panelist). (2010, July 27). Internet activists and authoritarian regimes: Who's winning? *The Foreign Policy Initiative*. Retrieved from http://www.foreignpolicyi.org/content/internet-activists-and-authoritarian-regimes-whos-winning

Websites

Cirius website. (2012). Retrieved from http://cirius.com/social-media-instant-messaging-rise-leave-email/

Digital Agenda for Europe website. (n.d.). *About the future Internet*. Retrieved https://ec.europa.eu/digital-agenda/en/about-future-internet

GILC website. (n.d.). Privacy and human rights: An international survey of privacy laws and practice. *Global Internet liberty campaign*. Retrieved from http://gilc.org/privacy/survey/intro.html

Internet World Stats website. (2014). Internet users in the world: Distribution by world regions - 2013 Q4. *Internet World Stats*. Retrieved from http://www.internetworldstats.com/stats.htm

Press Reference website. (n.d.). Retrieved from http://www.pressreference.com/Be-Co/China.html

Reporters without Borders website. (n.d.). Retrieved from http://surveillance.rsf.org/en/china/

Webopedia website. (n.d.). Retrieved from http://www.webopedia.com/TERM/N/narrowcast.html

Worldometers website. (n.d.). *Current world population*. Retrieved from http://www.worldometers.info/world-population/

Name Index